Cognitive Behavioural Couple Therapy

Cognitive behavioural couple therapy (CBCT) is an enhanced and contextually grounded approach that provides evidence-based strategies for working with couple distress, as well as individual psychopathology in the context of a distressed relationship. *Cognitive Behavioural Couple Therapy: Distinctive Features* explores this truly integrative and experiential way of working. This model has significantly widened the traditional CBT focus on cognition and behaviour to include an equal emphasis on emotion, stable individual differences and vulnerabilities, as well as an awareness of the importance of the environment and the wider context for couple relationships.

Comprising 30 key points, and divided into two parts – Theory and Practice – this concise book includes numerous clinical examples that illustrate the key features of CBCT. It will offer essential guidance for students and practitioners experienced in individual CBT, as well as practitioners of couple therapy from other theoretical orientations who require an accessible guide to the distinctive theoretical and practical features of this contemporary approach.

Michael Worrell is Consultant Clinical Psychologist and Director of Training at the London CBT Training Centre. He is a BABCP accredited Therapist, Trainer and Supervisor and delivers training in CBCT. He has presented at national and international conferences on training issues related to increasing access to CBCT. His previous publications have focussed on issues related to developing metacompetence in CBT and aspects of the therapeutic relationship.

Cognitive behaviour therapy (CBT) occupies a central position in the move towards evidence-based practice and is frequently used in the clinical environment. Yet there is no one universal approach to CBT and clinicians speak of first-, second-, and even third-wave approaches.

This series provides straightforward, accessible guides to a number of CBT methods, clarifying the distinctive features of each approach. The series editor, Windy Dryden, successfully brings together experts from each discipline to summarise the 30 main aspects of their approach divided into theoretical and practical features.

The CBT Distinctive Features Series will be essential reading for psychotherapists, counsellors and psychologists of all orientations who want to learn more about the range of new and developing cognitive behavioural approaches.

Titles in the series:

A Transdiagnostic Approach to CBT using Method of Levels Therapy by Warren Mansell, Timothy A. Carey, and Sara J. Tai

Acceptance and Commitment Therapy by Paul E. Flaxman, J.T. Blackledge, and Frank W. Bond

Beck's Cognitive Therapy by Frank Wills

Behavioural Activation by Jonathan W. Kanter, Andrew M. Busch, and Laura C. Rusch

CBASP as A Distinctive Treatment for Persistent Depressive Disorder by James P. McCullough, Jr., Elisabeth Schramm, and J. Kim Penberthy

Cognitive Behavioural Couple Therapy by Michael Worrell

Compassion Focused Therapy by Paul Gilbert

Constructivist Psychotherapy by Robert A. Neimeyer

Dialectical Behaviour Therapy by Michaela A. Swales and Heidi L. Heard

Functional Analytic Psychotherapy by Mavis Tsai, Robert J. Kohlenberg, Jonathan W. Kanter, Gareth I. Holman and Mary Plummer Loudon

Metacognitive Therapy by Peter Fisher and Adrian Wells

Mindfulness-Based Cognitive Therapy by Rebecca Crane

Narrative CBT by John Rhodes

Rational Emotive Behaviour Therapy by Windy Dryden

Rational Emotive Behaviour Therapy 2nd Edition by Windy Dryden

Schema Therapy by Eshkol Rafaeli, David P. Bernstein and Jeffrey Young

For further information about this series please visit
www.routledgementalhealth.com/cbt-distinctive-features

Cognitive Behavioural Couple Therapy

Distinctive Features

Michael Worrell

LONDON AND NEW YORK

First published 2015
by Routledge
27 Church Road, Hove, East Sussex, BN3 2FA

and by Routledge
711 Third Avenue, New York, NY 10017

Routledge is an imprint of the Taylor & Francis Group, an informa business

© 2015 Michael Worrell

The right of Michael Worrell to be identified as author of this work has been asserted by him in accordance with sections 77 and 78 of the Copyright, Designs and Patents Act 1988.

All rights reserved. No part of this book may be reprinted or reproduced or utilised in any form or by any electronic, mechanical, or other means, now known or hereafter invented, including photocopying and recording, or in any information storage or retrieval system, without permission in writing from the publishers.

Trademark notice: Product or corporate names may be trademarks or registered trademarks, and are used only for identification and explanation without intent to infringe.

British Library Cataloguing in Publication Data
A catalogue record for this book is available from the British Library

Library of Congress Cataloging in Publication Data
Worrell, Michael.
Cognitive behavioural couple therapy: distinctive features/Michael Worrell.
Pages cm. — (Cbt distinctive features)
Includes bibliographical references and index.
1. Couples therapy. 2. Cognitive therapy. I. Title.
RC488.5.W677 2015
616.89'1562—dc23
2014040960

ISBN: 978-0-415-72927-7 (hbk)
ISBN: 978-0-415-72928-4 (pbk)
ISBN: 978-1-315-72082-1 (ebk)

Typeset in Times New Roman
by Swales & Willis Ltd, Exeter, Devon, UK

For Maria, Tomas and Daniel.

Contents

Foreword ix
Preface xiii
Acknowledgements xv
Abbreviations xvii

Part 1 THE DISTINCTIVE THEORETICAL FEATURES OF CBCT 1

1. A distinctive focus: couple relationships and well-being 3
2. A distinctive history 7
3. Enhancements to CBCT 13
4. Micro behavioural factors 17
5. Cognitive factors in couple distress 1: attention, attribution and expectancies 23
6. Cognitive factors in couple distress 2: assumptions, standards and schemas 27
7. Emotions 31
8. Motivation and personality 35
9. Macro patterns: stability and change 39
10. Environmental influences on couple functioning 43
11. Contextualising 'difference' 47

12	Individual factors: psychopathology	53
13	The example of depression	57
14	A contextual model of couple functioning	61
15	Values and aims of CBCT	65

Part 2 THE DISTINCTIVE PRACTICAL FEATURES OF CBCT — **69**

16	The role and stance of the therapist	71
17	Assessment	75
18	Feedback and goal setting	79
19	Behavioural interventions: guided behaviour change	83
20	Improving communication: expressive and listening skills	87
21	Improving communication: decision-making conversations	93
22	Challenging cognitions: selective attention and attributions	97
23	Challenging cognitions: relationship standards and beliefs	101
24	Working with emotions	105
25	Working with the environment	109
26	Sequencing interventions	113
27	Addressing individual psychopathology: the case of depression	117
28	Infidelity and relational trauma	121
29	Ending issues	125
30	Conclusion: the challenges and possibilities of CBCT	129

References	133
Index	139

Foreword

Michael Worrell is an excellent author, clinician, trainer, supervisor and collaborator in the field of cognitive behavioural couple therapy (CBCT). Rarely do you find an individual who has this range of talents, and it is the integration of these skills that has led Michael to create such a thoughtful and valuable book on CBCT. I have worked in the couple field for 40 years, and almost every important aspect of couple therapy that I know and the wisdom of many other people, including Michael's unique insights, are contained in this volume. And what is more amazing is that he has presented it so clearly and concisely! As a reader, you are in for a real treat.

Like a skilled CBCT therapist, Michael understands that as an author, he is not lecturing or merely putting out ideas that are to be accepted by some unknown reader. He recognises that writing is an interpersonal process between the author and reader, and his role is to provide the structure, focus and general principles to build upon the reader's existing knowledge and understanding, so the reader can grow and be the most effective therapist possible. He begins by giving you a framework for understanding couples from a cognitive behavioural framework because this framework guides the conceptualisation that leads naturally into effective treatment planning. And while this conceptualisation is important, as a clinician you also need to understand a range of specific interventions that you might employ to address the complex situations that couples present. So this book gives you what you need in terms of understanding how to implement all of the major interventions that are currently available in the field of CBCT and how they can be used flexibly and adapted to a given couple's needs.

Over the past few years, I have had the opportunity to do peer supervision with Michael and some of our other colleagues. And having listened to his therapy sessions, I know he is a superb couple therapist himself. He knows what a therapist needs to understand, and as an experienced trainer and supervisor, he knows how to present it. A skilled couple therapist is adept at staying on track and not getting distracted even when it is tantalising to do so. This book stays on track; it is focussed and does not get distracted by interesting side issues. As a result, it says a lot in little space. And as a reader, you will benefit from Michael's breadth of knowledge in the couple and individual psychotherapy field. Thus, this volume is not a mere distillation of an individual's thoughts or a summary of one perspective. Instead, it integrates ideas and interventions from all of the approaches to couple therapy that have strong empirical support, along with Michael's own perspectives that are integrated with others' ideas; there are many new ideas here.

And this book does not attempt to simply describe complex clinical phenomena. For example, couples experiencing relationship distress often include one or both partners with notable individual psychological distress. Recognising that therapists will routinely be presented with this clinical complexity, Michael explains how couple-based interventions can be used to target individual distress as well as relationship concerns. And a particular highlight of the book from my perspective is the respect that Michael demonstrates for each couple and how culture and environment help to shape the couple's experience and are a vital part of treatment.

Although it might seem a bit off target to mention in the foreword to a professional book, you should know that Michael Worrell is an extremely fine, ethical human being with tremendous good will and a great sense of humor. Why is this important? Because just as you want to select a therapist who is professionally skillful, you also want to know that the therapist is well adjusted and a client can trust the therapist's perspective. Likewise, this book is not a list of intervention techniques; it is the thoughtful integration of theory, research and clinical practice presented by a person who understands and embodies healthy interpersonal relationships – you can trust this book.

So pull up a chair, get comfortable, and get ready for a good read. If you are like me, you are about to learn a great deal about intimate relationships and how to help people be their best in relationship with others, even when they are discouraged and can't see how to make it work. Here is a masterful discussion of applying well-documented cognitive behavioural principles to intimate, committed relationships.

Professor Don Baucom
University of North Carolina
August 2014

Preface

Cognitive behavioural couple therapy (CBCT) is by no means a recent arrival to the family of cognitive behavioural therapies. In the United Kingdom, however, it is currently experiencing something of a revival, due in part to its recognition by the National Institute for Health and Care Excellence (NICE) as a recommended treatment for depression, where depression is being maintained by a distressed couple relationship. The effectiveness of CBCT is by no means limited to depression, as ongoing empirical work is demonstrating that it can improve outcomes for individuals and couples struggling with a wide range of presentations, including both physical and mental health problems. It is within this context that the UK government's Increasing Access to Psychological Therapies (IAPT) programme has sought to improve the availability of CBCT through a substantial programme of training. I and my colleagues at the Central London CBT Training Centre have had the privilege of working closely with Professor Don Baucom from the University of North Carolina, one of the principal originators of this approach, in delivering this training and conducting research into therapists' experience of learning to become CBCT therapists, as well as their effectiveness in delivering this treatment to distressed couples.

For me, one of the most compelling aspects of CBCT has been the effort to develop a theoretical model, and evidence-based interventions, that are truly reflective of, and responsive to, the full complexity of couple distress and well-being. The approach is truly interpersonal, experiential and integrative in the best senses of these words. As a result, some of the best and clearest texts in this area are, well … long! Having immersed myself in this literature, it seemed to me that what is needed, particularly from the perspective of therapists new to the approach, is a relatively concise introduction to the model and its principal intervention strategies. The Distinctive Features series immediately struck me as the perfect vehicle for this task. Like other texts in this series, I have attempted to present the most important and distinctive features of CBCT in terms of 15 key theoretical points and 15 key practical features. The attempt to remain within this disciplined approach has been not too dissimilar to the struggle experienced by some partners in couple therapy (who may be prone to over-verbalising) when they are asked to 'speak in paragraphs' to give their partner a chance of hearing them. Frustrating but ultimately rewarding!

In my view, implicit within CBCT is recognition of what the Existential Therapists would refer to as the 'givens' of existence (Spinelli, 2007). This includes recognition of the fundamentally relational nature of human existence and that human relationships always exist within, and are not understandable apart from, a context. I hope that in my attempt to speak in paragraphs I have managed to communicate some of the complexity and comprehensiveness of this approach. At various points I have described a number of 'case examples'. These are all heavily disguised, altered descriptions of couples that I have worked with. These descriptions are in essence heavily edited constructed highlights used to illustrate a point, and cannot do justice to the full richness and complexity of any specific couple or individual.

Acknowledgements

I would like first and foremost to thank Professor Don Baucom from the University of North Carolina. His inspiring teaching and highly supportive and enlightening supervision has been the impetus for my continuing fascination for psychotherapeutic work with couples. Like all Master therapists he embodies the model in his way of being. In his teaching and supervision he likewise encourages others to find their own way of being a couple therapist in a manner that stays true to the principles of the model. This book represents my own attempts to achieve such an integration of fundamental principles with technical flexibility.

I would also like to acknowledge and thank my colleagues at the Central London Cognitive Behavioural Therapy Centre, and in particular Sarah Corrie, Ursula Barbieri, Rita Woo, Anna-Maria Smit, Louise Payne, Rita Santos, Holly Boulton and Effie Molyva. Thanks also to Philip Tata for having the foresight and energy to get the ball rolling on so many projects, not least of which has been the project of widening access to CBCT in the UK. Finally, I would like to thank the couples who have chosen to work with me as a therapist, for sharing their struggles and teaching me directly about the challenges and possibilities of working with distressed relationships.

Abbreviations

BCT	behavioural couple therapy
CBT	cognitive behavioural therapy
CBCT	cognitive behavioural couple therapy
DBT	dialectical behaviour therapy
EFCT	emotion-focussed couple therapy
IAPT	Increasing Access to Psychological Therapies
IBCT	integrative behavioural couple therapy
IOCT	insight-oriented couple therapy
NICE	National Institute for Health and Care Excellence

Part 1

THE DISTINCTIVE THEORETICAL FEATURES OF CBCT

A distinctive focus: couple relationships and well-being

Psychological therapies are increasingly concerning themselves with the issue of 'well-being'. One of the biggest factors accounting for any individual's sense of well-being is the quality of their interpersonal relationships. Couple relationships, as a subset of important interpersonal relationships, are one of the most central domains in which people seek a meaningful and rewarding life. Hahlweg et al. (2010) assert that whilst rates of marriage in western countries have declined since the 1970s, and rates of divorce and separation have risen, it remains the case that, across cultures, most people become involved in an intimate couple relationship at some stage in their lives. The recent developments in recognising the validity of same-sex marriages testifies to the importance that individuals and cultures continue to place on long term committed couple relationships.

Why do couples seek the services of a therapist? Gurman (2008) states that the most common concerns centre around issues of emotional disengagement and weakening commitment, struggles around power and control, communication difficulties, issues of infidelity, sexual issues, role and value conflicts and issues involving abuse. Couples may also present to a therapist where one or both partners is experiencing a significant degree of psychopathology such as depression, anxiety and substance misuse problems.

'Couple distress' has been found to have a strong and reciprocal relationship with individual psychopathology. To take the example of depression, it has been found that the presence of couple distress is a significant risk factor for the development of depression in one or both partners (Beach et al., 2008). Additionally, the presence of depression in one or both partners is a risk factor for the development of relationship distress (Halford et al., 1999).

Relationship distress and psychopathology can be mutually reinforcing. This relationship is by no means restricted to the case of depression, as it has been found that a wide range of differing forms of psychopathology, as well as physical health problems, are negatively impacted by relationship conflict and distress (Snyder and Whisman, 2003). Relationship distress can be understood as a broad, often chronic, interpersonal stressor that may act as a triggering and maintaining factor for vulnerable individuals to experience forms of psychopathology.

Given this bi-directional influence, it is reasonable to suggest that a focus on alleviating individual symptoms of psychopathology may have a beneficial effect on subsequent relationship distress. Unfortunately, the empirical findings to date do not support this (Whisman and Baucom, 2012). Whilst these interventions may result in the reduction of individual symptoms, this does not generalise to an improvement in relationship functioning and satisfaction. Rather, it has been found that the presence of relationship distress is a poor prognostic factor for the success of treatments that target individual psychopathology. Individually based therapies may not be effective where couple distress is present as they do not directly address this (Whisman and Baucom, 2012).

The evidence that couple therapy, of various orientations, can be effective is impressive. Over 100 clinical trials have demonstrated the efficacy of various forms of couple therapy with the most substantial evidence having been demonstrated for cognitive behavioural forms of couple therapy (Snyder et al., 2006). Intriguingly, in the case of depression, couple therapy can be effective in reducing couple distress *and* improving levels of depression in one or both partners (Barbato and D'Avanzo, 2008; Whisman and Baucom, 2012).

CBCT proposes that couple distress can be usefully understood and addressed at two levels:

1. Primary distress: This is understood to be the distress that arises where partners are unable to successfully resolve issues that can be traced to their patterns of similarity and difference in terms

of basic needs and motives. Partners may experience problematic differences, for example, in needs for closeness versus needs for autonomy. Such differences can become problematic over time as the couple is challenged to adapt to changing life circumstances.
2. Secondary distress: This is understood as the distress which develops as a consequence of the couples' ineffective interactions, which are expressions of their efforts at coping with and resolving primary distress. Secondary distress often leads couples to feel hopeless regarding the possibility of resolving primary sources of distress and is most immediately encountered by the therapist in the form of the couple's expressions of hostility and withdrawal.

CBCT addresses both primary and secondary sources of couple distress. CBCT is distinct from both individually focussed forms of CBT and non-CBT approaches to couple therapy in a variety of ways. The form of CBCT being presented here can be considered to be both an 'enhanced' and an 'integrative' model that seeks to do full justice to the complexity of couple relationships. Rather than seeking to 'reduce' our understanding of couple distress and well-being to the role of cognition (or any one alternative factor), the model has expanded its scope to include a wider range of interacting domains (Baucom et al, 2002).

In addition to these distinctive conceptual aspects of CBCT, there are important aspects of the practice of CBCT that can be highlighted. These include:

- The model is 'principle' based. Due to the complexity of work with couples, it is not realistic to present the model in a highly manualised session-by-session format. Cognitive behavioural work with couples calls for therapist flexibility and ability to adapt interventions in response to the couple's in-session responding in a way that embodies its central principles.
- An active-directive therapist style. Whilst allowing for differences in therapists preferred style, work with couples calls for the ability to compassionately, and at times assertively,

intervene, in order to manage the overall structure of the session and to maintain a focus on key intervention targets. Maintaining this stance and avoiding a range of pitfalls (such as siding with one partner or giving them a disproportionate amount of time in session) is part of the art of CBCT.

For the therapist, CBCT can be both challenging and rewarding. It is an effective intervention for reducing couple distress and improving couple well-being, as well as an effective strategy for working with individual psychopathology in cases where this is affected by, and in turn affects, the couple relationship.

… A DISTINCTIVE HISTORY

A distinctive history

This chapter describes the principal historical antecedents to the form of CBCT presented in this book as well as the main influences from other CBT and non-CBT models of couple therapy.

Traditional behavioural couple therapy (BCT)

Traditional BCT first emerged in the 1960s as part of the broader project to apply the principles of classical and operant conditioning to clinical problems. Authors such as Stuart (1969) applied Exchange Theory as well as classical and operant conditioning and Social Learning Theory and proposed that distressed couples could be distinguished upon the basis of observable differences in the frequency of exchange of positive and negative behaviours.

BCT emphasised the detailed functional analysis of micro level interactions. That is, present interactions in specific contexts. These analyses revealed sequences of mutual reinforcement and punishment that are responsible for maintaining couple distress. Interventions were designed to help partners define, shape and reinforce desirable behaviour in highly specific operationalised terms. The traditional BCT model also posits that couple distress may be maintained due to the partners not having developed, or failing to utilise, specific behavioural skills of communication (Jacobson and Margolin, 1979). BCT includes procedures to assist couples in learning these skills within therapy sessions, combined with homework assignments to assist in generalisation and maintenance of these skills into the couple's normal environment.

The use of skill training as well as the detailed functional analysis of couple interaction patterns has been maintained in CBCT.

However, an exclusive focus on behavioural skills building has been found to be too restrictive to account for the complexity of couple distress and couple interaction.

Cognitive therapy

Cognitive therapy emphasises that individuals' behavioural and emotional responses are mediated by cognitive content and processes (Beck et al., 1979). Given that intimate relationships are very frequently a focus for both emotional distress and behavioural difficulties, cognitive therapists have applied the cognitive hypothesis to relational distress in a highly productive fashion.

Cognitive therapists such as Beck (1988) and Dattilio (2010) have identified a range of cognitive content (beliefs and assumptions, such as 'In order for me to be happy you should never be angry with me!') and processes (selective attention, catastrophising) and explored how these influence couple distress and satisfaction. As will be discussed in Chapters 5 and 6, CBCT has significantly developed the cognitive understanding of couple distress and satisfaction

Social cognition

The field of social cognition, a program of research within social psychology and not tied primarily to the clinical domain or to 'abnormal psychology', has explored a range of social-cognitive processes that are important in understanding the maintenance of couple distress as well as couple satisfaction. CBCT has developed a number of these insights and applied these to distressed couples. This development is described more fully in Chapter 5. Two clear examples of this are the work on 'attributions' and 'schemas'. Attributions refer to the theories people generate to account for the causes for their own and others' behaviour, such as 'The reason you are late is that you want to avoid spending any time with me!' Schemas refer to long-standing and stable fundamental beliefs about the self and relationships, such as 'My relationships inevitably fail as I am not worthy of being loved'.

Acceptance and mindfulness

At the same time as Baucom, Epstein and colleagues were formulating CBCT, Jacobson and Christensen (1996) were developing a revised cognitive behavioural model that also sought to overcome the perceived limitations of a purely behavioural model. Their model of 'integrative behavioural couple therapy' (IBCT) proposes that all relationships will include areas of incompatibility between partners that are not amenable to change and that it is frequently the couple's persistence in seeking to change these areas that is responsible for the maintenance of distress. This approach includes both behavioural strategies intended to help foster change in those areas that are amenable to this, as well as 'acceptance' strategies focussing on those factors that are not.

There are substantial areas of overlap between CBCT and IBCT in both theory and practice, and in their evolution they have also clearly informed and influenced each other. One area of difference is the relative importance placed on the notion of 'acceptance' in IBCT. In this model, acceptance is viewed as a primarily emotional experience and one that often mediates positive therapeutic change. For CBCT increases in acceptance of differences within a couple relationship are seen as a likely outcome of cognitive and behavioural changes (Baucom, 2014, personal communication).

IBCT can rightly be regarded as an evidence-based approach to couple therapy (Christensen et al., 2004). A range of other contemporary CBT approaches have also been presented that emphasise processes of acceptance and mindfulness in couple functioning and distress. Acceptance and commitment therapy, or ACT (Hayes et al., 1999) is a contextual behavioural science approach that has recently been extended from individual therapy to couple therapy interventions (Harris, 2009; Dahl et al., 2013). Additionally, mindfulness-based CBT approaches have recently been extended for work with couples (Gehart, 2012).

Non-CBT-based approaches: emotion and insight

There are a great number of approaches to work with couples. Few of these have been subjected to the degree of empirical testing necessary to be regarded as being evidence-based approaches. Two non-CBT approaches are significant, however, in that they have gained some evidence for effectiveness. These approaches also offer distinctive points of emphasis that in turn have influenced the evolution of CBCT into its current 'enhanced' version.

Emotion-focussed couple therapy (EFCT)

EFCT is an integration of core philosophical assumptions and strategies from humanistic-experiential therapies with concepts from Systems Theory and Attachment Theory. Developed by Johnson and Greenberg (1985), the approach privileges the role of emotion in organising partners' subjective experiences and behavioural responses to each other. The approach provides an important corrective to the over-emphasis on cognition and behaviour to be found in earlier cognitive-behavioural approaches. The model makes substantial use of Attachment Theory (Bowlby, 1989) and proposes that couple distress can be understood primarily in terms of 'insecure' attachment styles and difficulties couples experience in understanding and responding to each other's attachment needs. Whilst eschewing direct attempts at behavioural skills building, the EFCT therapist uses strategies to assist each partner in communicating their own attachment needs and emotions more clearly as well as responding empathically to the attachment needs of their partner. It is assumed that improvements in partners' ability to recognise and respond to their own and their partners attachment needs will lead to constructive behaviour change in the relationship.

Insight-oriented couple therapy (IOCT)

Whilst BCT, CBCT, IBCT and EFCT place a relatively greater emphasis on present interaction patterns in understanding couple distress, insight-oriented couple therapy, or IOCT (Snyder and Wills, 1989), consistent with its psychodynamic base, places emphasis on the role of past developmental processes for each individual in the relationship. The approach emphasises the importance of each partner developing insight into both their own and their partner's developmental history and how current couple distress is related to defensive strategies each partner has learned, to avoid the activation of emotional states associated with past hurts. This model assumes that insight into these individual developmental factors will facilitate, through a process of 'affective reconstruction', the dropping of unhelpful defensive strategies in the current relationship. Partners are aided in differentiating past from present relationships and developing more helpful strategies for interacting with their partner in the present.

Enhancements to CBCT

This chapter discusses a number of key domains that have been integrated into the enhanced CBCT model, to provide a more flexible and complete model of couple distress and functioning.

Emotion

Whilst behavioural and cognitive behavioural approaches to couple therapy have not ignored the role of emotion, typically emotion had been relegated to a secondary status, and was seen as an outcome of behavioural or cognitive processes. Consistent with developments in the field of CBT more generally, the enhanced model of CBCT now places an equal emphasis on the role of emotional factors and includes interventions focussed on working directly with emotions in therapy. As will be discussed in Chapters 7 and 24, CBCT includes a range of interventions that may be focussed on assisting partners to manage excessive and unregulated emotion, as well as assist in learning skills to more effectively identify and communicate emotional experience as an important source of information about personal needs and values. This increased emphasis on emotion is consistent with some of the propositions of EFT from which CBCT has drawn helpful concepts as well as technical strategies. This increased focus on emotion is also consistent with recent work in CBT where problems with dysregulation of emotions are seen as a central maintaining factor for psychopathology (Linehan, 1993).

A micro and a macro level focus

Earlier versions of CBCT tended to emphasise a tight focus on 'micro' level behavioural interactions as well as the effects of specific cognitive content and processes. This micro level focus has been highly productive and continues to remain a feature of this approach. This perspective has been significantly enhanced, however, by an additional focus on more 'macro' level themes in couple distress.

One example of this has been an increased emphasis on understanding what each individual brings to the relationship from their developmental histories. This, in some respects, is consistent with the emphasis of IOCT in identifying what is 'carried forward' by each partner in order to facilitate behavioural, cognitive and emotional change. Whilst not understanding such factors from a psychodynamic perspective, long-term personality patterns as well as relatively stable individual differences in basic motivations and needs (such as the need for closeness versus distance and the need for individual achievement versus the need for affiliation with others) are seen as important factors to consider, both in assessment and treatment. These individual difference variables can include 'normal' variations in personality and temperament, as well as longstanding patterns that are implicated in individual psychopathology.

Environment

Cognitive behavioural approaches to couple therapy have always included a focus on the couple's environment, as this is a basic principle of all behaviourally derived approaches. More cognitively focussed models of individual therapy have, on occasion, been criticised for what has been perceived to be a too exclusive focus on phenomena going on inside the client's head and ignoring very real sources of stress and challenge in the client's wider world. The enhanced model includes an increased focus on broader aspects of a couple's environment. The environment can frequently be understood in terms of a source of stress and demand to which the couple needs to work effectively as a team to respond to. Additionally, the environment may be understood in terms of actual or potential sources of support and resource in assisting the couple to meet both individual and relational needs. This increased emphasis on interaction with the environment can be seen as partly reflecting the influence of systemic models of couple functioning.

Culture

An appreciation for how cultural factors affect both individual and couple functioning is crucial in the enhanced model of CBCT. This model has also been referred to as a 'contextual' approach in order to emphasise this increased focus on environmental, cultural and other factors that are wider than just a focus on micro level couple behavioural interaction. Cultural factors are always present in any couple therapy and CBCT practitioners need to be able to understand how such factors influence all aspects of the model including, for example, how cultural factors influence couple expectations and beliefs about how the relationship should function as well as assumptions about how men and woman should and do behave and what behaviours are considered normative and non-normative.

A balance of positive and negative

Older versions of CBCT tended to emphasise interventions designed to decrease the frequency and severity of negative behaviours and cognitions in a couple's relationship. Whilst the importance of reducing negative factors has been maintained, the contemporary model has placed a far greater emphasis on identifying and increasing positive behaviours, emotions and cognition. This is consistent with the general trend within CBT to emphasise client resilience and strengths and also partly reflects the challenge presented from 'Positive Psychology' that has criticised traditional approaches for being too narrowly focussed on the elimination of 'symptoms' or the removal of problems (Snyder and Lopez, 2007). The enhanced contextual model of CBCT includes an equal emphasis on increasing positive aspects of couple functioning and strengthening couple relationships as well as reducing identified problems.

In the following chapters of Part 1, the primary domains that are considered of importance in CBCT are reviewed, including those traditionally associated with the approach, such as micro behavioural factors, as well as those domains that have recently been integrated into the model.

Micro behavioural factors

Couples seeking therapy frequently exhibit high rates of negative interactions and behaviours and low rates of positive interactions and behaviours (Epstein and Baucom, 2002; Gottman, 1994). However, the relationship between positives and negatives is not best characterised as being a simple one-dimensional continuum, as there are a range of possible patterns of negatives and positives. Perhaps the most typical presentation is that of the frequently angry and arguing couple where there is indeed an overall low frequency of positives and a high frequency and intensity of negatives. Also problematic is a pattern whereby there is both a low level of positive behaviours and a low level of negative behaviours. These are relationships where the partners complain that the relationship feels 'empty'. Additionally, some relationships may be characterised by a high level of both positive and negatives such that their interaction is best described as 'stormy'.

In broad terms, CBCT aims to help couples reduce the frequency and intensity of negative behaviours (in order to reduce levels of couple distress) as well as to increase the frequency and range of positive behaviours (in order to increase couple satisfaction and well-being). Epstein and Baucom (2002) have introduced a range of distinctions and concepts that are of great use in assisting couple therapists to assess and intervene at a behavioural level.

Communication and non-communication behaviours

Communication behaviours are concerned with interactions that involve the expression and reception of thoughts and feelings as well as the resolution of practical problems or demands.

Non-communication behaviours may involve both instrumental acts (doing the dishes, paying the bills) as well as expressive acts that partners exchange on an ongoing basis (such as doing favours for each other). Such instrumental acts often, in addition, do communicate important meanings between partners; however, these are frequently implicit.

Positive behaviours

Empirical evidence strongly supports the notion that high levels of couple satisfaction are associated with a high frequency of positive behaviours and interactions. What is meant by 'positive' from a behavioural perspective? The experience of a behaviour or interaction as positive clearly implicates the meanings that partners attach to these behaviours. Nevertheless, positive behaviour can be usefully described at behavioural level. Epstein and Baucom (2002) argue that a distinction can be made between 'expressive' positive behaviours and 'instrumental' positive behaviours. Expressive positive behaviours may include those that signify caring, love and affection as well as expressions of approval, the sharing of humour and positive physical touch. The functions of such behaviours may include establishing and maintaining emotional connection, intimacy, providing and receiving reassurance, soothing and care. Instrumental positives on the other hand are behaviours that ensure that the partners are able to meet the demands of life such as earning money, paying bills, making repairs to the house and making financial decisions. Such instrumental behaviours may also function to provide the partners with a sense of 'We-ness' or a sense that they are a good team who can function effectively in the world.

Epstein and Baucom (2002) argue that both positive and negative behaviours can be understood in terms of their focus or the way in which they are directed. Partner behaviour can be understood as focussing upon 'the other', the couple as a unit, on the 'self' as well as on the environment. Any particular behaviour may also have multiple focus points. Forms of positive behaviours also vary in terms of their frequency and impact. A trip to Venice to celebrate an important couple anniversary may function to revitalise a relationship that has begun to be experienced by both partners as flagging or having become routine. Such a positive behaviour is likely to be infrequent and its impact is in fact related to its relative novelty. Just as important are the higher frequency day-to-day positives such as one partner kissing the other before leaving for work in the morning.

Negative behaviours

Negative behaviours may also be described in terms of their focus upon the self, the partner, the couple relationship and the environment, with a single behaviour or class of behaviours frequently impacting across focus points. The most researched class of negative behaviour in the couple therapy field has been negative communication behaviours. Not all instances of negative behaviours are problematic for a relationship. Indeed, a superficially calm relationship in which arguments never occur can be problematic as relationships need to be able to include the expression and processing of inevitable conflict (Wile, 1993). What then makes a negative behaviour or interaction problematic? Epstein and Baucom (2002) suggest that negatives can come to have long-term undesirable consequences through two main ways:

1. Frequent negative interactions create an overall negative 'atmosphere' in the relationship in which it is difficult for the partners to feel as ease with each other and to turn to each other to meet their needs.
2. Particularly impactful forms of negative behaviour such as criticism, contempt, disgust and hostility function to lower the self-esteem of one or both partners.

Epstein and Baucom (2002) argue that negative behaviours often arise from several sources. First, partners may be unaware of the impact of their negative behaviours upon their partner and the relationship. Due to a range of reasons, such as selectively attending only to their partner's negative behaviour and attributing the cause of difficulties only to the partner, there may be significant deficits in self-monitoring as well as deficits in skills for changing their own negative responses. Second, partners may have learned to use negative communication styles as a strategy for meeting their own needs or as a strategy to terminate negative behaviours from the partner. For example, shouting loudly for attention may be experienced by one or both partners as negative; however, it may also be effective and as such be reinforced and maintained. Third, negative behaviours may be understood as being related to individual psychopathology.

Behavioural interaction patterns

In addition to analysing discreet forms of negative and positive behaviours, couple researchers have identified repetitive patterns of behavioural interaction that have been found to be implicated in the generation and maintenance of couple distress. These include:

1. Negative reciprocity: This is the tendency of one partner to respond to the other partner's negative communications with further negatives that sets up a self-perpetuating cycle of negatives (Gottman, 1979). Whilst *positive reciprocity* also exists, it appears that negative reciprocity is more impactful and directly related to couple distress.
2. Mutual attack: Partners are engaging in reciprocal cycles of aggressive behaviour including criticism, sarcasm, verbal threats and abuse as well as physical abuse.
3. Demand-withdraw: One partner approaches and pursues the other, frequently in an assertive or aggressive manner, and the other partner responds by withdrawing physically and/or emotionally. As one partner withdraws, the other responds with further demand and approach behaviours, which results in yet further withdrawal behaviours in a self-perpetuating cycle.

4. Mutual withdrawal: Both partners engage in distancing behavioural manoeuvres that function to allow both to avoid aversive interactions and emotional states.
5. Mutual and unilateral disengagement: This is often a very challenging presentation for the therapist as one or both partners have effectively disinvested emotionally in the relationship. One or both partners are no longer looking to the other as a source of potential need satisfaction and may report being emotionally empty or disconnected.

Cognitive factors in couple distress 1: attention, attribution and expectancies

Janice has worked hard all afternoon on various household tasks, in an effort to be available to Greg when he returns home. As he arrives home, the first thing he notices is a pile of papers on the kitchen table. 'Why is this house always such a mess?' he states loudly. Janice says nothing and thinks, 'He always does this! He obviously isn't interested in spending any time with me, he just wants a maid.'

It is not possible to understand the impact of any specifically 'negative' or 'positive' form of partner behaviour without reference to the interpretations and meanings that are ascribed to that behaviour. Cognitive behavioural therapists and researchers have identified a wide range of cognitive processes as well as forms of cognitive content (such as beliefs, rules for behaviour, assumptions) that are related to emotional distress and forms of psychopathology. All of these are of potential relevance to the practice of CBCT in as much as they may throw light upon important factors operating within one or both of the individuals. CBCT theorists have in addition identified forms of cognitive process and content that appear to be very commonly related to couple distress, both in cases where there is significant individual psychopathology and in cases where individual psychopathology is absent or less significant.

This chapter focuses on how cognition affects the way partners may respond to specific events occurring in their relationship, including how partners 'pay attention' to aspects of a situation, how 'causality' is attributed and how this may then relate to 'expectancies' for what may happen in the future.

Selective attention

An individual's attentional resources are always limited and as such partners will in most circumstances pay attention to, notice and process certain aspects of a situation whilst ignoring others. This essentially adaptive process can have unfortunate consequences, including the finding that partners may have a low level agreement regarding the question of whether or not a specific event even occurred. For example, Jacobson and Moore (1981) found that partners had an agreement rate of less than 50 per cent regarding whether specific events had or had not occurred during a 24-hour period!

Selective attention can frequently function in a biased manner such that an individual focuses only on negative aspects of their partner or an event, to the exclusion of positive aspects, thereby maintaining negative emotional responses and behavioural reactions (Beck, 1988). Equally, an individual may ignore negative aspects and only focus on positive or neutral information. Helping partners notice the effects of selective attention and learning to exert some control over this normal cognitive process must not be done at the expense of validation and understanding of the effects of actually occurring negatives. Some of the challenge, of course, arises from the fact that both a high frequency of actual negatives may be present, in addition to a pervasive pattern of selectively attending to aspects of these negatives in a biased fashion.

Attributions

In addition to attending in a biased manner, people also create interpretations about *why* events occur. This is particularly the case when this concerns other people's behaviour. People in effect generate theories about the reasons why others have behaved in particular ways, and the nature of these theories has an important impact on their subsequent cognitive, emotional and behavioural reactions. In couple relationships, the question of 'why you behaved the way you did' is often crucial. Couples researchers have found that the pattern of attributions in distressed couples, often expressed as 'blaming', is similar to the pattern of attributions found in depression (Epstein, 1985). That is, attributions are ascribed to the partner's behaviour which are negative, global, internal to the other, and stable. For example: 'The fact that you have come home late is simply because you don't care about me or this relationship, you are an unfeeling slob whose only interest is sport and beer'. Positive behaviours of the partner are in turn attributed to external and temporary factors: 'You only brought flowers because the couple therapist said you should, you are just trying to distract me'.

Expectancies

Attributions also serve as the basis for the construction of predictions, or expectancies, regarding how people are likely to behave in the future. Learning how to predict and anticipate others' behaviour is essential for navigating the social world. The difficulty, as always, is where these expectancies are overly biased (in either a positive or negative manner) and inflexible such that, in the case of couple distress, this can generate experiences of hopelessness about future possibilities for change: 'You never listen to me! You are just not capable of it due to being emotionally illiterate and it's pointless me trying to get through to you!'

As well as resulting in negative emotional responses and increases in couple distress, negative attributions and expectancies are likely to result in partners struggling to communicate with each other. There is often a self-fulfilling pattern such that selective attention provides information that the negative attributions and expectancies are correct, resulting in an escalation of negative mood states which further biases attention in a negative cycle. The resulting increase in negative reciprocity further entrenches each partner's attributions and expectancies regarding the other.

Cognitive factors in couple distress 2: assumptions, standards and schemas

The previous chapter discussed forms of cognition that may be implicated in couples' emotional and behavioural responses to specific events. Cognitive behavioural theorists and researchers have also given considerable attention to more implicit forms of cognition that can be regarded as 'deeper', 'broader' and more reflective of early developmental history. CBCT theorists have also given attention to these forms of cognition and in particular have focussed on 'assumptions', 'standards' and 'schemas'.

Assumptions

Assumptions are cognitions that partners hold about how themselves, others and relationships *are*. They are beliefs about how the world of relationships actually operates and may reflect culturally based notions, for example, of how males and females are different (Baucom and Epstein, 1990). This might include assumptions such as 'men are unable to relate emotionally' or 'women are naturally better at caring for children'. A particularly important class of assumptions is the beliefs that an individual holds about their partner, which may include what their values are, how they tend to behave and how they experience the world. This could be expressed, for example, as 'my partner likes things to be ordered and predictable, she's a bit of a perfectionist'. Such assumptions provide a basis for making both attributions as well as constructing expectancies about the partner's behaviour and reactions. Gordon and Baucom (1999) have suggested that they are a number of assumptions that appear to be generally associated with the success of a long-term intimate relationship. These concern assumptions that the partner is reliable, honest and trustworthy. Behaviours that violate such assumptions, such as infidelity, lead to particularly severe forms of couple distress and relationship crises. In addition, the presence of couple distress over a period of time can itself function to challenge the assumptions an individual holds about themselves, their partner and the relationship. Partners may state: 'I don't like who we have become in this relationship and I don't like how I am in this relationship'.

Standards

Whilst assumptions are beliefs regarding how things actually are, 'standards' refer to beliefs about how things 'should be' (Baucom and Epstein, 1990). A crucial question concerns whether a partner's assumptions concerning how things actually are match up with their beliefs regarding how things should be. Again, often reflecting both social-cultural factors and family of origin, standards can be held regarding a wide range of aspects of intimate relationships. This can include standards for the other: 'my partner should always be caring and put my needs first'; 'my partner should share most of my interests'. Standards may also be maintained about what sorts of contact are appropriate with the wider social environment: 'we should both desire to spend most of our free time with each other', 'our couple relationship is a greater priority than our relationship with our parents' or 'children always come first and us as a couple second'.

Epstein and Baucom (2002) have suggested that couples experience a greater degree of well-being to the extent that they experience that their assumptions of how things are in their relationship is consistent with how things should be, regardless of the specific content of these standards. However, there is also some evidence that couples experience higher degrees of relationship satisfaction and well-being to the extent that they maintain 'relationship-oriented standards'. That is, that they maintain standards that assert the importance of prioritising their couple relationship, that the relationship should be one of closeness and sharing and that decision making and role taking should be based on values of equality between partners. At the same time, they assert that standards often reflect deeply held values and that the goal of CBCT is not to advocate for the couple taking on specific values but rather assisting them to clarify the range of both positive and negative consequences that arise from the standards that they do hold.

A related issue is the degree to which one or both of the partners has reflected upon and clarified their relationship standards and the extent to which relationship standards are or are not an important part of an individual's way of construing the world. Whilst for some individuals the questions of 'how would I like and expect my relationship to function? What is important to me in terms of relationship with my partner?' may have been an issue that has received considerable reflection, for others such standards have been constructed and maintained at a more implicit, taken-for-granted level. There are also individual differences in the extent to which standards may be rigidly versus flexibly maintained and the degree of emotional distress associated with having relationship standards challenged.

Schemas

A number of cognitive behavioural theorists have utilised the concept of 'schema' to account for the ways individuals can be seen to automatically process information about the world in a biased fashion. Jeffery Young's (1990) 'Schema Focussed Therapy' has developed this concept further and has identified a range of schemas that are frequently implicated in forms of individual psychopathology. To the extent that many of the identified schemas have a clear interpersonal element (such as 'I am worthless and others are rejecting') the identification of such has a clear relevance to couple therapy, particularly in cases where couple distress and individual psychopathology co-maintain each other (Dattilio, 2010).

Epstein and Baucom (2002) have identified a particular type of 'schematic information processing' that has direct relevance for couple interactions. These authors suggest that individuals vary in the extent to which they process the world in relational terms; that is, the extent to which they pay attention to and interpret information in terms of 'self in relation to other' or in terms of 'we'. This has been termed 'relational schematic processing' as opposed to 'individual schematic processing'. Individuals high in relationship schematic processing will tend to interpret events, and make predictions about the likely impact of their own behaviour, in terms of consequences for their relationships. Individuals high on individual schematic processing will tend to become absorbed in their own experience and activity and may fail to process the impact of this upon their partners. Epstein and Baucom (2002) have suggested that increases in relational schematic processing, particularly for individuals relatively low on this when they enter couple therapy, may mediate successful outcomes in CBCT as well as other forms of couple therapy.

Emotions

The experience and expression of emotion is central in both couple well-being and couple distress. In initial sessions, couples will frequently describe their difficulties in terms of how these make them feel, or in terms of how previously valued emotional experiences of closeness and warmth have been lost. Couple distress is frequently encountered by therapists in the form of high frequency and high intensity negative emotions such as anger and hostility, as well as forms of 'detachment' or shutting down. Couple therapists may encounter partners' sadness, guilt, shame, anxiety, jealously and depression. Equally, when partners are asked what first drew them to each other, they will very often report that a significant factor was how being with the other person made them feel. They may report having felt a sense of belonging, of love, connection and 'rightness' about the relationship.

Emotional experience

There are a wide range of factors that may influence the degree to which each partner experiences specific emotions. Epstein and Baucom (2002) have argued that it is important to make a distinction between the emotions that a partner may experience in response to a specific event and their consistent levels of positive versus negative affectivity. That is, there are stable individual differences in levels of affective experiencing that over time interact to affect the overall emotional tone of a relationship. People who are temperamentally high on positive affectivity and low on negative affectivity are likely to shape a couple relationship in a more positive overall direction.

Equally, individuals high on negative affectivity are likely to shape the relationship towards an overall negative tone.

Partners' experiences in their earlier relationships are also likely to significantly influence what is brought forward into the current relationship in terms of emotional experiencing. Some individuals have experienced earlier relational environments in which emotional expression between family members was poor or highly dysregulated. As a result, these individuals may not have developed skills for accurately recognising and labelling their own emotional experience. The history and developmental stage of the current relationship is also important, particularly where couple distress has been present over a long period of time. In this situation an overall negative emotional atmosphere may 'colour' currently occurring events such that the partners' emotional responses often seem both very rapid and frequently disproportionate to the triggering event. Alternatively, partners may have effectively 'checked out' or disengaged from the relationship, such that there is very little happening emotionally.

Emotional regulation

Individuals differ in the strategies they have developed for regulating the experience of emotion. Many individuals find the experience of negative emotions difficult to tolerate and use a range of strategies, such as avoidance and distraction, to lessen their experience of these emotions. Again, due to important developmental factors, partners may have deficits in skills for soothing and regulating their own emotions as well as skills for helping their partner soothe and regulate their emotions.

Gottman (1994) has shown how some individuals will use strategies such as withdrawing from an interaction, or 'stonewalling', as a means of reducing the intensity of negative emotional states that are triggered by conflictual interactions. Gottman (1994) also found that a typical pattern in couple distress is that of one partner criticising and the other becoming defensive or counter-attacking. These behaviours may serve a wide range of functions, one of which may be reducing distressing emotional experiences. Partner behaviours that express contempt and criticism, whilst potentially functioning to create distance, have been found by Gottman (1994) to be particularly problematic for the maintenance of couple distress.

Emotion-focussed therapists (Johnson, 2004; Greenberg and Goldman, 2008) have also argued that an important strategy partners use for dealing with distressing emotions is to change a distressing emotion into a different emotion. Johnson and Greenberg (1995) introduced a useful distinction between *primary* and *secondary* emotions. In this model, primary emotions are understood to be biologically adaptive in that they help orientate the individual to the significance of triggering events in terms of their basic needs and goals. For Johnson (2004) the primary emotions are principally related to an individual's 'attachment' needs and concern a biologically based drive to experience 'connection', security, warmth and intimacy. Secondary emotional responses, often in the form of anger, shame and anxiety, are understood as being triggered as a result of primary emotional responses being frustrated.

This distinction between primary and secondary emotional experiences is similar to the distinction between 'hard' and 'soft' emotions made by Christensen et al. (1995). In this model 'hard emotions' are those that display strength and dominance while 'soft emotions' express vulnerability. Christensen et al. (1995) argue that soft emotions always accompany hard emotions and that in couple therapy it is important for therapists to help partners recognise and express their softer underlying emotions. Epstein and Baucom (2002) have argued that some of the hard or secondary emotions may be related to needs for power and control and that these needs can be understood as separate from the need for attachment and security.

Emotional expression

Factors that impede or facilitate the experience and regulation of emotion are also likely to influence the expression of emotion. It is often through the expression of emotions to a partner that emotional experience can be moderated and relational needs met. In some cases a partner may show skill deficits in terms of ability to express emotions to their partner. This may be related to deficits in being able to notice and correctly label emotional experience as well as difficulties in expressing emotions in a modulated fashion, such that it is possible for the partner to receive the communication that is presented. Some people may struggle differentiating their emotions and communicating these in a manner that would facilitate an appropriate response, or the communication may be presented at a level of intensity that is either too intense or not clear enough to allow for the partner to appropriately respond. Individuals that struggle with issues of poor emotional regulation often express emotions in an overly intense and undifferentiated manner (Fruzzetti, 2012). In these cases it can also be difficult to differentiate between the high degree of emotional distress that is fairly common in couple distress from dysregulated expressions of emotion that are traceable to individual deficits in this domain.

Cognitions and emotions

In addition to difficulties with the experiencing, regulation and expression of emotion, partners may present with cognitions *about* emotions that affect their functioning in all three of these areas. Leahy (2002) has proposed a model of 'emotion schemas' which describes how individuals may maintain beliefs, rules and standards regarding the experiencing, regulation and expression of emotions that may lead to significant difficulties in terms of forms of individual psychopathology as well as relational distress. Beliefs such as 'my emotions are uncontrollable and dangerous', 'my emotions do not make sense', 'others will respond badly to my expression of emotion', 'I should never feel anger', etc., are important to assess for each partner both in terms of what they may have individually brought into the relationship as well as what rules, assumptions and standards may have evolved through their interaction that characterise what forms of emotional experiencing and expression are allowed and encouraged versus those forms that are disallowed and punished.

Motivation and personality

Cognitive behavioural therapies typically focus more on the question of *what* is occurring in a problematic situation as opposed to *why* the situation has occurred. This traditional focus has been highly productive as it has led to the identification of a wide range of cognitive and behavioural factors that are involved in the maintenance of forms of psychopathology. CBCT has sought to extend the focus on what is occurring in couple interaction to also include the question of why problematic patterns of couple interaction have arisen. Clinical observations suggest that couples frequently present with repetitive interaction cycles such as 'demand-withdraw' and 'negative reciprocity' that are triggered by, and are expressive of, key areas of conflict and tension in the relationship. This may include, for example, conflicts over the degree of intimacy desired, or the degree of individual autonomy seen as necessary by one or both partners. These sources of conflict may be related to what each individual brings to the relationship in terms of their relatively stable motives and personality styles (Epstein and Baucom, 2002). Clinicians can assist partners in understanding the reasons for some of their key struggles by assisting them to clarify how their individual differences in these areas are implicated.

Motives and relationship tensions

Employing motivational concepts, which involves propositions concerning 'basic needs', is novel for cognitive behavioural approaches. Epstein and Baucom (2002) have incorporated concepts from McClelland (1987), who understands 'motives' to consist of cognitive schemas, emotional arousal and behavioural repertoires directed towards meeting goals and needs. Epstein and Baucom (2002) note that motives that are strongly implicated in couple relationships can include those involving *approach* as well as those related to *avoidance*. Approach motives can be further divided into those that are directed towards 'communion' or 'connection' with others and those that are directed towards 'individuation' or 'separateness'. This notion of a continuum between drives towards connection to others versus drives towards separateness and individuation is a very common one in the literature on motivation across differing theoretical perspectives and could be argued to point towards a basic 'existential tension' inherent in human relationships (Spinelli, 2007).

The motive to connect to others can be further delineated into a number of sub-themes. This differentiation in communally oriented motives is important, as two people who are strong on this general motivation of connecting with others may not be similar in all its sub-themes. Epstein and Baucom (2002) argue that there are four communally oriented motives that may be important in couple relationships. These include the motive towards *affiliation* (a need to associate with others rather than be alone), *intimacy* (a need for contact and mutual self-disclosure), *altruism* (a need to take care of and give to others) and *succorance* (a need to receive care from others). As noted, two individuals high on motives towards 'connection and belonging' will not necessarily meet along all dimensions, and their experience of couple conflict may be traceable to differences along this dimension. Tanja and Steve are both highly social individuals who love going to parties. They frequently have arguments after leaving these social gatherings, as Steve is highly interested in meeting and talking with as many people as possible, moving easily from one group to another (a high motive for affiliation). Tanja often feels let down and left alone by Steve at these events, as what she most desires is that they would navigate these social encounters as a couple and that Steve would strive to include her in all the interesting conversations he has with these people (a high need for intimacy and succorance).

Individually oriented motives, in contrast, can include a motive towards *autonomy* (the desire to move freely in the pursuit of individual interests and goals), *power* (the motive to exercise influence and to have an impact on others and the environment) and *achievement* (the motive to perform at a high standard in a chosen domain). Again, whilst it may be clear how partners with substantial differences in individually oriented motives may experience difficulties (although this is by no means inevitable!), partners who have substantial similarity in these motives may also find themselves experiencing conflict as they go through various phases in their development as a couple.

Epstein and Baucom (2002) also note the existence of motives that are focussed upon the avoidance of experiencing psychological or physical discomfort. It is important to distinguish between these motives as, for instance, an individual who appears to be motivated to spend a lot of time separate from their partner may be doing so more from a wish to avoid the discomfort of experiencing anxiety or anger in the relationship rather than due to a positive need for individually focussed behaviour.

Personality styles

'Personality styles' can be understood as an additional class of individual dispositions that may account for the degree of consistency shown in partners' behavioural, emotional and cognitive responses across situations and across time. As is the case with motives, differences between partners in personality style may on the one hand complement each other (and may often be the basis of initial attraction and bonding between partners) as well as potentially lead to consistent areas of conflict and distress. A wide range of personality factors have been studied and many of these have potential relevance for understanding couple functioning. Whilst not advocating the necessity for a thorough assessment of individuals with a battery of personality tests, Epstein and Baucom (2002) encourage clinicians to assess how each partner may express aspects of the 'Big 5' personality traits that have received a high degree of empirical support in the literature. These well-established personality traits include:

1. Extraversion-introversion: degree of sociability, need for stimulation and adventures
2. Agreeableness: including degree of trust and altruism
3. Conscientiousness: needs for order, competence and achievement
4. Neuroticism: degree of emotional instability and tendency to respond with negative affect
5. Openness to experience: curiosity and embrace of novelty.

9

Macro patterns: stability and change

Previous chapters have outlined how the traditional BCT focus on micro patterns of behaviour, stemming from ideas of social exchange, has been significantly widened by a focus on cognition, emotion and the role of individual partners' needs and personality styles. CBCT has argued that, in order to better understand the 'why' of relationship distress, it is important to understand each partner's needs and personal goals and how they seek to fulfil these in their relationships. Such an understanding can help couple therapists identify commonly occurring themes in couple distress and the repetitive behavioural patterns that maintain these difficulties. This chapter returns to the domain of behaviour but does so from a broader perspective; that is, macro level behavioural patterns that can be understood to be relatively stable patterns of behaviour that are linked to the fulfilment of needs for communion as well as individuality.

Epstein and Baucom (2002) have argued for the incorporation of concepts from Systems theory as well as an awareness of the typical developmental challenges couples experience in attempting to maintain a relationship that successfully fulfils both their individual needs and preferred ways of being. Systems theories (Nichols and Schwartz, 2001) describe how the survival of a couple relationship can be understood in terms of the need for *homeostasis*, or a balance between stability and change. On the one hand, relationship well-being is dependent upon the maintenance of macro level patterns of behaviour that maintain a needed degree of *stability* and consistency in meeting partners' needs. On the other hand, couple relationships require flexibility in order to allow *adaptation* to normative and non-normative developmental changes. The normative developmental challenge of the birth of a first child frequently challenges couples' abilities to adapt in order to continue to meet each partner's needs at an acceptable level. Helping the couple understand the stresses bearing on their relationship, as well as providing a context in which they can have conversations to explore how each partner is experiencing this developmental change and clarifying and negotiating issues related to standards and expectations for support and role division, may help the couple successfully adapt.

Whilst couples may develop a wide range of idiosyncratic behavioural macro patterns, Epstein and Baucom (2002), drawing on the literature of Family Therapy (Minuchin, 1974; Bennett and Wolin, 1990), have identified several common forms of macro patterns that are involved in couples' efforts to both maintain stability and adapt to change.

Rituals

Jason and Steve have been partners for 10 years. They both lead busy lives and have a high achievement orientation as well as a high level of motivation for affiliation. They have a wide circle of friends that they see regularly. Friday night, however, is 'curry and DVD night' and nothing is allowed to interrupt this. They take turns choosing the DVD as they have different tastes but this is hardly the point. The importance of Friday night is its predictability and the sense of closeness and exclusivity it provides. No friends have ever been invited to come over to watch the DVD or have dinner as it is implicitly understood that this is for them as a couple only. Neither one of them can remember how this pattern started or how they had come to the decision to keep doing this. It is simply 'what we do'. Rituals, as forms of repetitive behaviour, can function to maintain the stability of a relationship as well as support partners by providing a 'touchstone' as they navigate various developmental challenges and needs to adapt over time.

Boundary maintenance

The concept of 'boundaries' is an important one in the family therapy literature. Family therapists such as Minuchin (1974) have argued that a healthy couple relationship is characterised by relatively 'permeable' boundaries. A permeable boundary is said to be present where there is clear communication between the partners and where it is possible to successfully balance both needs for intimacy and belonging and needs for individual activity outside of the relationship. Epstein and Baucom (2002) have argued that many of the strategies used in CBCT, such as activity scheduling both individually and as a couple, communication training to share feelings and make decisions as well as interventions to clarify and modify standards, can be viewed as functioning to help couples establish and maintain a permeable interpersonal boundary around the relationship.

Social support

The maintenance of a relationship that successfully meets individual needs for both belonging and autonomous functioning frequently includes partners providing each other with forms of social support. There are wide forms of specific micro behaviours that may have the function of providing support to a partner, such as providing information, providing encouragement and esteem support, facilitating access to wider forms of environmental support, etc. A key issue involves an individual's preferences for types of support and how this may change over time as part of normal development. Additionally, specific forms of support may be needed in response to novel challenging situations. When Janice is stressed at work what she prefers is for her partner Susan to gossip with her about how dreadful some of her colleagues are. What she needs when she is preparing for a job interview, however, is some direct feedback on how her CV is looking.

Environmental influences on couple functioning

Graham and Shannon have been together for 5 years. They describe themselves as always having had a stable and supportive marriage. They are living in a crowded housing estate, after Graham experienced health problems and lost his job. Their two children are doing well at school but they are often worried about their physical safety on the estate. Graham is depressed and feels he has let his wife and family down. They have few social contacts and live an isolated life. They describe escalating couple distress and worsening mental health for both of them.

As a behavioural approach, CBCT has always considered the impact of environmental factors. Epstein and Baucom (2002), however, have proposed that environmental factors need to be given increased importance in understanding couple functioning and couple distress. They suggest that the systemic perspective on couples can be particularly helpful, in that it conceptualises the couple system as always contextualised within a range of other larger, interlocking systems including, for example, the extended family systems of both partners, work contexts, community institutions and wider social and cultural systems.

Epstein and Baucom (2002) propose that the impact of the environment on couple functioning can be understood in terms of the manner in which environmental factors may function as *demands* as well as the extent to which environmental factors exist as *resources* for the couple. As was outlined in the previous chapter, these demands and resources exist as a range of factors that both challenge and support the homeostasis of the couple system.

Environmental demands

Considerable empirical evidence confirms that adverse environmental demands are associated with the onset and maintenance of couple distress (Wright et al., 1994). Epstein and Baucom (2002) distinguish between demands that have a direct versus an indirect effect on couple distress. In the example above, Graham and Shannon's daily interactions are directly affected by the chronic stress of living in an environment characterised by deprivation and a risk of violence to themselves and their children. Indirect effects of environmental demands can be seen in the example of Graham losing his job. The loss of self-esteem experienced by Graham due to the loss of a previously highly valued role also results in a worsening of couple distress. Graham may be struggling to structure and manage his time and his worsening mood is expressed through his often critical and negative comments to Shannon regarding how she maintains the house.

Demands may also have negative effects via the interference in previously rewarding macro behavioural patterns. For example, having to move to a deprived area may result in a loss for Graham and Shannon of previously rewarding rituals (such as going to the cinema every Tuesday evening) that had functioned to provide a sense of connection and intimacy. Additionally, such demands may impact upon the boundaries that are being maintained around the couple. In the example here, there has been a hardening of the boundary between the couple and the environment that can be partly understood as a functional defensive withdrawal from a hostile environment. Some environmental demands may have the result of weakening the boundaries around a couple. Thus, should Graham and Shannon come to depend upon Shannon's extended family for financial support, the intrusive demands made by Shannon's father (for example) for detailed information regarding the couple's spending may increase couple distress.

Environmental resources

A couple's environment may also provide needed resources including financial support, social support and instrumental support. A common example is parents providing assistance with babysitting, allowing a couple to maintain rituals for 'couple time'. This could also include social support in the form of helpful advice and emotional support around the challenges of caring for young children. Community organisations such as churches, schools and leisure centres can also provide forms of support that reduce the level of demand experienced by the couple system to meet all of the individual partners' needs, as well as assisting the couple to meet their joint communally oriented needs. The input received by Graham and Shannon from their children's school in continuing to support their development appears to be one of the few environmental supports available to the couple and their family system. Therapeutic intervention for this couple may involve assisting them to access a wider range of environmental resources.

Cognitions regarding environmental demands and resources

Whilst it is important for the couple therapist to include an assessment of the couple's environmental demands and resources, such an assessment must take into account each partner's cognitions and emotions regarding these. Consistent with general CBT principles, the degree to which any particular environmental factor is experienced as a demand or a resource is likely to be influenced by how these are appraised by the partners concerned. These appraisals in turn are likely to reflect broader social-cultural factors regarding what types of environmental demands and resources are seen as normative and desirable. Graham and Shannon may maintain relationship standards concerning independence of the couple system from family of origin. Thus, whilst the offer of financial support from Shannon's family is in one way an environmental support, the intrusive questioning from Shannon's father about their finances functions as an environmental demand, due to the fact that it leads to the perception of an important standard for the couple relationship being violated. Some cultural groups maintain different expectations and standards for involvement with extended family which would result in this form of environmental support being welcomed without distressing implications of the couple having 'failed'.

Contextualising 'difference'

CBCT requires couple therapists to pay attention to the potential relevance of a wide range of contextual factors. Culture, ethnicity, gender, sexual orientation and other domains of 'difference' have an impact on individual, couple and environmental factors and how these in turn influence couple distress and well-being (Fischer et al., 2014). Conceptually, as aspects of the wider context for couple relationships, such factors form part of what might be thought of as 'the horizon of understanding' (Moran, 2000). As is elaborated further in Chapter 14, 'the horizon' is a concept borrowed from existential philosophy and refers to the wide array of 'background' assumptions, beliefs and practices that both limit the way behaviour and events can be understood and also provide a basis for making sense of events such as 'becoming a couple' or 'separating' as cultural practices that are in a sense experienced as 'the way things are'. Aspects of a couple's horizon can be brought to awareness and are also subject to challenge and change rather than being fixed.

Culture and ethnicity

Cultural and ethnicity factors are relevant to all aspects of the CBCT model of couple functioning. Individually focussed CBT interventions for anxiety and depression have been adapted for the needs of differing cultural groups (Hinton and La Roche, 2014). There is, by contrast, less work that has been done that can support couple therapists in adapting therapy for specific cultural and ethnic groups (Fischer et al., 2014).

As Hays (1996) has argued, theories of psychological intervention themselves can be seen as expressing implicit culturally based values. For example, as Sevier and Jean (2009) note, the types of training in communication skills undertaken in CBCT express the value of partners clearly stating, in a direct and open fashion, areas of difference and conflict in the relationship. Fowers (2001) makes a similar argument and suggests that many of the strategies used in couple therapy reflect 'old-fashioned virtues' first put forward in ancient Greek philosophy. Such virtues include self-restraint (self-regulation), generosity, honesty, courage, equality and commitment. Whilst these virtues may be valued in many cultural contexts, this can at times be inconsistent with some cultural expectations for how conflict should be dealt with. In contrast to western cultural contexts that place a greater value on individualism and clear statements of difference, some Asian cultural contexts place a greater value on social harmony and encourage partners to express disagreements in a more indirect way that does not result in any individual 'losing face' or experiencing shame and embarrassment (Lee and Mock, 2005; Markus and Kitayama, 1991, Sevier and Jean, 2009). At the same time, it cannot be assumed that this will automatically be the case when seeing couples from such a cultural background. Some authors have found that once couples experience acculturation to a westernised context, they are more likely to value direct expressions of difference (Flores et al., 2004).

Other domains where cultural factors may impact on aspects of the CBCT model include variations in the manner in which emotions are expressed in relationships, expectations regarding the degree of boundaries around the couple relationship and connections with wider extended family, as well as standards and beliefs about how power is negotiated in relationships (Sevier and Jean, 2009).

Cultural factors may also affect the way in which couples respond to the type of active and directive therapeutic stance taken by the couple therapist. Some authors (Vera et al., 2002) have argued that such a stance is often more appropriate for ethnic minority clients; however, this lacks empirical support and cannot be assumed. Bhugra and De Silva (2000) have argued that couple therapists need to attend to cultural differences, as power differences are inherent to all therapeutic relationships, and that such relationships always reflect the broader socio-political context. There is some research indicating that ethnic minority groups may experience heightened levels of relational distress and that this can be related to a range of stressors that disproportionately affect couples, such as unemployment, racism, poverty and violence (LaTaillade, 2006). For black and other ethnic minority clients living in a white majority culture, for example, racism may be a constant chronic stressor on their couple relationships that is not immediately or easily foregrounded for discussion, particularly in instances where the therapist is themselves a representative of the white majority culture.

CBCT requires therapists to conduct a detailed idiosyncratic assessment of each couple and to function in a contextually sensitive manner, which includes an expectation for cultural competence. This requires therapists both to be knowledgeable about cultural factors of relevance for the clients they see, as well as being highly collaborative with specific couples and open to exploration of how cultural factors may be important in understanding the extent to which the interventions offered in CBCT are appropriate or may need to be modified.

Gender

The impact of gender has received more attention in the literature than cultural factors. For example, Epstein and Baucom (2002) have suggested that 'relational schematic processing' or the tendency to process information in terms of its potential impact and relevance for relational concerns, may mediate successful outcomes in couple therapy. Several studies have found gender differences in degrees of relational schematic processing whereby, generally, females are found to be higher on this form of processing as compared with males. Additionally, studies have found that improvements in relational schematic processing are related to successful outcomes where these improvements are demonstrated by the male partner (Epstein and Baucom, 2002). That is, both female and male partners experience

49

greater relationship satisfaction when the male partner makes gains in relational schematic processing.

Gender differences have also been studied at a behavioural level. For example, the commonly observed 'demand-withdraw cycle' has been found to be frequently demarcated along gender lines such that males are more frequently observed to enact the 'withdraw' pattern and females the 'demand' role (Gottman, 1994). Additionally, some studies have shown that males frequently experience a higher degree of physiological reactivity during conflictual conversations. It has been suggested that the greater tendency for males to use withdrawal and avoidance may be partly a behavioural strategy to manage this higher level of physiological discomfort experienced during such conversations (Gottman, 1994). However, some studies have also suggested that the demand-withdraw pattern may express a functional control strategy related to issues of power, in that the partner who uses withdrawal more frequently effectively blocks efforts at achieving change in areas with which they are happy with the status quo. When the conversation concerns domains in which the male is seeking change, the demand-withdraw pattern has been observed to operate on the reverse gender pattern (Epstein and Baucom, 2002).

Sexual orientation

Much of the research conducted on couple functioning completed over the past several decades has focussed primarily on married heterosexual clients, thus there is further work to be done exploring how such findings are generalisable to or have limited applicability to same-sex couples. Same-sex couples frequently experience considerable environmental stress in the form of an understandable and realistic fear of discrimination from a 'heterosexist' cultural context, as well as isolation from forms of environmental support (Long and Andrews, 2011). CBCT therapists need to educate themselves about the struggles faced by such couples and work in as flexible and collaborative a manner as possible to assess the range of individual, couple and environmental factors at play for specific same-sex couples. Long and Andrews (2011) argue that couple therapists need to be aware of the realities of institutionalised discrimination faced by same-sex couples, and to avoid the error of assuming that the differences between same-sex and opposite-sex partners are so extreme that no comparison is meaningful, as well as the error of ignoring differences between these groups that do exist. The first of these errors may lead therapists to assume that the couple distress being experienced by a same-sex couple can be attributed to the very fact that they are a same-sex couple. The second error may lead therapists to underestimate and to fail to account for specific challenges experienced by same-sex couples.

Individual factors: psychopathology

The existence of psychopathology in one or both partners can present significant challenges for couple therapy (Snyder et al., 2003). An individual's vulnerability to, or current experience of, forms of psychopathology may be implicated in a variety of ways in couple distress. First, the presence of couple distress may act as a stressor, triggering and maintaining forms of individual psychological distress. It can be challenging for the clinician to distinguish this from the heightened emotional dysregulation characteristic of couple distress. Second, the presence of psychopathology in one or both partners may negatively impact on the relationship, interfering with the satisfaction of individually and communally oriented motives, thereby triggering and maintaining couple distress. There is now a large body of literature that links problems in couple relationships with forms of adult psychopathology and suggests that relationship distress and individual psychopathology mutually influence one another (Whisman and Uebelacker, 2003).

It is essential that the CBT couple therapist assesses for the presence of individual psychopathology that potentially pre-dates and transcends the distress attributable to difficulties in the couple relationship. Additionally, it is important to assess the manner in which couple distress and individual psychopathology mutually impact upon each other. Conducting such an assessment may help determine the extent to which successful couple therapy may lead to a lessening of individual psychopathology, and to what extent it may be necessary to target individual psychopathology, either during couple work or in a separate individual therapy.

The effects of individual psychopathology on couple distress

An individual's experience of psychopathology may detrimentally affect couple functioning in a variety of ways. This may include changes in interaction patterns that have occurred as ways of coping with symptoms. Baucom et al. (2003) describe how couples may 'rearrange' their relationship in order to accommodate one partner's experience of psychopathology. Such efforts at rearranging the relationship reflect processes of 'homeostasis' described in earlier chapters. A common example of this is where partners may make concessions to, and unwittingly reinforce, varieties of avoidance behaviours. For example, one partner may have experienced a traumatic incident, such as a car accident, that results in the experience of symptoms of post-traumatic stress, including flashbacks and nightmares and a pattern of avoidance of previous activities related to driving. In addition to the loss of functioning for the affected individual, the partner may act to support them by taking on all driving-related tasks and assisting them to avoid situations that may trigger anxiety. This additional level of demand on the supporting partner may, particularly if extended over time, lead to the onset, or feed into the maintenance of couple distress. A similar pattern may occur where an individual has a long-term phobia, such as a phobia of birds, where the supporting partner may spend an inordinate amount of time searching through magazines to remove pictures of birds in an effort to lessen the distress experienced by their partner. A further example is the not uncommon situation of an individual with obsessive compulsive disorder who repeatedly makes demands on their partner to clean their hands or clothes before coming into the house, or to refrain from touching certain objects in the house due to this triggering the individual's obsessions. Again, in such a situation the individual's psychopathology functions as an additional source of demand on the relationship, makes the relationship less rewarding and potentially feeds back into the maintenance of the individual psychopathology.

As well as interfering with couples' behavioural patterns, individual psychopathology may function to create an overall negative

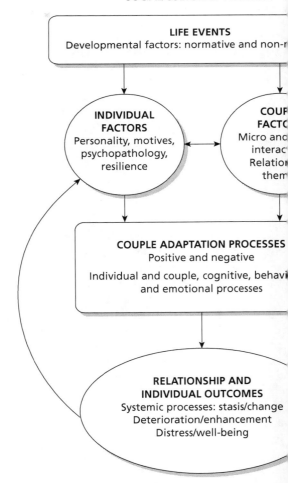

Figure 14.1 A contextual model of couple functioning

A model of couple functioning

have outlined a range of domains and factors that
must be taken into account in order to adequately
nesis, maintenance and alleviation of couple dis-
se various factors related to each other in a fashion
y integrated perspective to emerge? A number of
ented models to address this. Halford (2001) pre-
c model' of the influences on couple relationships
features with the 'Adaptation Model' proposed by
om (2002). Both models set out how individual,
onmental factors interact as couple relationships
and meet with various normative and non-norma-
challenges. The Adaptation Model of Epstein and
lso integrates insights from Systems Theory and
'stress and coping' literature. The model provides
rk when assessing and formulating client difficul-
g treatment priorities. It's a framework that allows
entify client strengths and resources, located both
uals, the couple relationship and their wider envi-
potentially be drawn upon in therapy.

w is a 'Contextual Model of Couple Functioning'
oth the model of Halford (2001) and Epstein and
his model maintains the general schema presented
nd the relationships they argue exist between the
This model also highlights the wider context for
ps as constituting a 'horizon' for what might 'show
ationships. The 'horizon' is a concept borrowed
henomenological and hermeneutic perspectives
ls taken-for-granted implicit assumptions, beliefs
t provide a social-historical background for the

had a child, Susan maintains standards around the [chi]ldren come first'. From her perspective, Jason is [below] this standard and has become 'selfishly focussed on

[Su]san, in a state of chronic couple distress, have in [batted down t]he hatch' on the relationship, hardening the boundaries between th]emselves as a couple and the outside world, including [exten]ded family. In part this is due to a sense of shame [about Jason's d]epression. They were always seen as 'the high [functioning coup]le' and are unwilling to call on others for support. [A further c]onsequence of this is that both are experiencing a [lack of posit]ive contact with the environment which further acts [to maintain Jason's d]epression as well as Susan's experience of being [overwhelmed. Su]san is currently at risk of developing a significant [depression und]er herself.

[Targeting coup]le distress as a way to [manage individ]ual depression

[From a longitud]inal perspective, couple distress appears to dou[ble the likelihood] that at least one partner will experience a major [depressive disord]er over a 12-month period. Perhaps even more sig[nificantly, it has]been found that the presence of couple distress is [linked to in]creased risk for relapse following successful treat[ment for depressi]on (Whisman and Baucom, 2012). CBCT, it may [be argued, is a vi]able treatment option for couples such as Susan and [Jason as it has] the potential to improve both Jason's experience [of depression (vi]a interventions that target relationship distress) and [act as a buffer]ing to prevent a worsening of Susan's mental health [whilst reducin]g the risk of relapse for Jason via the lessening of

child or in terms of support and interest regarding S
challenges. Jason, who has always turned to Sus
for emotional support, does so increasingly, ofte
for support with problem solving and wishing to '
about work. This has severely taxed Susan's resou
herself experiencing increasing frustration and rese
perspective, he neither appears to use her advice
nor is he available to listen to her own concerns. S
has been forced to carry the load of running the fa
more is anxious that she has 'lost' Jason, as he no
be motivated to pursue the interests they both had

Effects on couple functioning

Depression is highly likely to have a range of ne
the couples' interactions with each other. As noted
ters, couple communications can focus both on t
thoughts and feelings, in order to promote the e
nection and the experiences of intimacy and emc
well as conversations directed at solving problems
sions. Depression may function to interfere with p
to engage in these forms of communication effec
find it increasingly difficult to listen to Susan w
her own concerns, hearing this inaccurately as bo
demand on him as well as an implicit criticism of
a result he 'tunes out' and does not accurately take
ing. Additionally he 'opts out' of any decision ma
solving around issues that involve their couple re
these decisions to Susan. On the one hand, doing s
on the other, his awareness that he is doing so furt
confidence and increases his ruminative thinking
'failed in life'. Jason's statements about 'feeling
interpreted by Susan as evidence of his 'rejectio
child, as somehow being insignificant to him.
never had explicit conversations about what the

13

of depression

*n describe a relationship that had, for most of its
characterised by a mutually rewarding pursuit of
cess and enjoyment outside of work. Couple dis-
pear until after the birth of their first child and
hen Jason experienced significant work pressures.
always prone towards a more 'negative outlook'
depressed for the past year and they both com-
ationship having become 'empty' and often char-
les of negativity and hostile withdrawal.*

ed in the previous chapter, the presence of sig-
l psychopathology can negatively affect each
uals, as well as negatively affecting the couple's
ach other and their environment. The example of
cularly common and it is worth highlighting how
l depression in one or both partners can be mutu-

dual functioning

lual is experiencing depression, it is likely that
npact on both partners' ability to meet their indi-
nunally oriented needs. Jason's withdrawal and
nterfere in both partners' ability to have needs for
ation met with each other. Jason's self-focussed
ans that he is unavailable to Susan and does not
notional and instrumental support, as he had done
for meeting demands at home with their young

borderline personality disorder, where difficulties
attachments are part of the essence of this presen
increase the couple's vulnerability to experienci
response to a wide range of stressors. Once in a sit
couple distress, the individual's coping strategies
taxed and many of these coping strategies (emc
forms of self-harm, etc.) may themselves lead to a
ple distress. Couple distress is highly likely to a
schemas around abandonment, for example, as v
individual's already poorly developed skills in em
Such individuals present difficulties for couple tl
individual may struggle with interventions such a
training and may require additional interventions
learn emotional regulation skills (Fruzzetti and Fa

wers the threshold for negative interaction cycles.
otional factors are also clearly important as it can
distressing to experience one's partner suffering
particularly if these are difficult to understand. A
respond with hostility, where negative attributions
g the individual's problems, such as 'they are los-
s well as expectations that the partner 'should be
f it'. The hostility that is expressed in response to
may further impact the individual's psychopathol-
g of their self-esteem and also contribute to couple

ouple distress on individual
jy

ave embarked upon couple relationships with a
rms of psychopathology that may have been 'sub
 stages of their relationship. The onset of couple
 of chronic stress, may lower the threshold for the
rt symptoms. This is consistent with Beck et al.'s
heory which states that individuals may present
ore beliefs and schemas that function as a vulner-
the onset of psychological problems in response
'matches' the content of these cognitions. Thus,
 present with core beliefs around 'abandonment'
rivation' that do not lead to significant problems
nship where things are running smoothly. With the
ip distress, however, triggered by their partner's
ig emotional unavailability following their being
om their job, for example, these underlying cogni-
 active, further exacerbating the extent of couple
g to significant individual psychopathology.
 present with difficulties consistent with patterns
sorder' may present with particular challenges
. The presence of a personality disorder, such as

development of couple relationships (Moran, 2000). Shared assumptions and cultural practices surrounding notions of 'romance', 'marriage', 'affairs' and 'life partners' are examples of aspects of the social/cultural horizon. The horizon, whilst taken for granted as 'the way things are', is not fixed and can become subject to challenge such as recent developments in recognising the validity of same-sex relationships. The horizon both provides the context for allowing events to be understood and responded to and also limits possibilities for understanding and action.

Following Epstein and Baucom (2002), the model proposes that a couple system (like other systems such as a family or organisation) needs to maintain a balance between the maintenance of current roles and patterns of behaviour and the flexibility to change and adapt to both expected and unexpected demands and challenges, be they positive (such as the birth of a planned child, or a partner gaining a new job), or negative (the illness of a child or partner). Characteristics of both individuals (including emotions, thoughts, personality factors and motives), the couple (characteristic communication and other behavioural patterns) as well as aspects of the environment (offering both demands and resources) function as both potential resources and sources of resilience and flexibility as well as sources of vulnerability for the production of couple distress and difficulties in adaptation.

This model allows therapists to formulate the struggles currently being experienced by a couple, including both 'micro' and 'macro' aspects, as well as placing the couple's current relationship difficulties within the larger context of the evolution of their relationship over time. The possibility that demands on the couple system will lead to enhancement over time is also accounted for. An example of this might be the arrival of a first child which is typically associated with a reduction in couple satisfaction as well as significant readjustments to partner roles. Depending on a wide range of factors, including individual characteristics of each partner as well as the availability of environmental resources, such a normative developmental demand is as likely to lead to enhancement of couple satisfaction over time as it is to deterioration.

15

Values and aims of CBCT

Many individually focussed forms of CBT have as their principle concern the elimination of symptoms of psychopathology and propose little in terms of what healthy functioning of the person might look like. Whilst avoiding holding up any model of what a couple relationship 'should look like', particularly in terms of factors such as specific relationship standards, CBCT does allow a perspective on functional and flourishing couple relationships (Baucom et al., 2011). Such a perspective is helpful not only in terms of specifying interventions that can help alleviate couple distress but also in terms of identifying factors that can improve couple well-being and resilience.

From the perspective of CBCT, a functional couple relationship is one that contributes to the health and well-being of both partners and in which both partners are able to work together as a team and relate to the wider environment in an adaptive fashion (Baucom et al., 2004). A key notion is that a healthy couple relationship will function to facilitate each partner's satisfaction of their individually and communally focussed motives. Such a relationship contributes to each individual's development and growth both in terms of career and educational aspirations as well as 'personal growth' and maturity. Additionally, a well-functioning relationship will serve as a major source of both emotional and practical or instrumental support in meeting daily demands as well as at times of significant stress or challenge. Such relationships are also able to adapt and change in response to both expected and 'normative' challenges (such as the birth of a first child) as well as in response to non-normative challenges (such as the unexpected redundancy of one partner from their work).

CBCT clearly embodies values of 'equality' in that it is suggested, on the basis of the available research, that a healthy relationship is one in which both partners will contribute to the well-being of the relationship and 'invest' in its maintenance and development over time. Couple relationships in which there is a relative balance of power and influence appear to be more functional than those in which there is a clear imbalance. The ability of both partners to communicate effectively in order to share their subjective experiences and to create intimacy, in addition to communicating to solve problems and make decisions, is seen as vital.

Whilst acknowledging the limitations of the current evidence base, in that this has been focussed mainly on heterosexual white married couples, the model seeks to support the functioning of other forms of couple relationship such as same-sex couples as well as seeking to work in a culturally competent way with couples from a wide variety of cultural contexts.

The model also suggests that functional couple relationships are ones in which each partner maintains relationship-focussed standards. That is, each partner holds beliefs regarding the importance of the couple relationship and the need of each partner to support the relationship. The concept of 'relationally schematic processing' has been proposed as a possible mediating factor for successful outcomes in couple therapy.

The aim of the CBCT therapist is to seek to establish a strong therapeutic relationship with each partner and the couple in order to collaboratively work with them to understand how the current experience of couple distress is being maintained and what the origins of this, in terms of individual, couple interaction and environmental factors, may be. CBCT then seeks to work with each individual and the couple as a unit to make changes to their patterns of interaction, their cognitions about themselves, each other and the relationship, and the manner in which they experience and express emotion as well as how they respond to environmental demands and access environmental supports, in order to reduce the current experience of couple distress and improve the resilience of the couple relationship. The CBCT therapist seeks to flexibly respond to the couple and to integrate and balance the use of cognitive, behavioural and emotional interventions depending upon the overall needs of the couple as well as their current state in a given moment in the therapy.

Consistent with the effort to include broader relationship themes or 'macro' factors in addition to the traditional BCT focus on 'micro' level behavioural changes, the CBCT therapist works with couples to set both specific goals for their relationship, such as to establish and maintain a regular night out each week to focus on increasing enjoyment as a couple, as well as setting broader goals such as 'increasing a sense of connection and intimacy in the relationship' which may be expressed in a wide variety of specific ways depending upon contextual factors.

The realities of work with couples is such that there are not infrequent occasions where, even with partners' willingness to attempt behavioural, cognitive and emotional changes, the best course of action for one or both partners is to seek to end the relationship. Such outcomes, whilst often a source of significant stress and distress for the parties concerned, need not necessarily be considered 'failed therapies'. Ultimately, the aim of CBCT is to assist couples in making good decisions about their relationships and the extent to which it is possible for their relationships to support the meeting of both partners' needs. Additionally, the decision to end the relationship does not necessarily entail the decision to immediately end the couple therapy as CBCT may be used to help individuals end their significant relationships in a manner that causes as little additional stress and distress as possible and is expressive of each individual's values.

Part 2

THE DISTINCTIVE PRACTICAL FEATURES OF CBCT

The role and stance of the therapist

Working with couples in distress can often be highly challenging for the therapist. The nature of couple distress is such that the therapist may frequently be working with couples who bring to the session a high degree of hostility and anger towards each other. It can be difficult to help such couples to contain their high levels of distress and overt hostility during the session in order to engage in therapeutic tasks relevant to key variables maintaining the distress. On the other end of the spectrum are couples who present as disengaged and shut down, where there may be an absence of either positive or negative affect. The therapist here may have to work very hard to activate and engage the partners in working on their relationship. An additional common dilemma for couple therapists, regardless of orientation, is the interpersonal 'pull' that may be experienced to align with one partner as the 'victim' or 'more rational and reasonable' partner, as opposed to the other partner. This can result in poor engagement, hostility or withdrawal from the partner who experiences themselves being aligned against by the therapist. This common dilemma is related to the broader reality the therapist is required to work directly with couple distress and interaction patterns 'live and in the room'.

In response to these and other challenging aspects of working with couples, the cognitive behavioural couple therapist needs to strive towards maintaining a therapeutic stance characterised by both flexibility and balance.

Flexibility

Baucom et al. (2008) describe the multiple roles the cognitive behavioural couple therapists may need to adopt during the course of therapy including that of director, educator, facilitator, collaborator and advocate. Particularly during the early stages of therapy, and especially where couples may be experiencing and expressing a high degree of emotional dysregulation during session, the therapist must be comfortable in the role of director, assertively intervening in unhelpful interaction patterns and directing partners' attention towards more useful therapeutic tasks. However, simply 'taking control of the session' and determining what will be focussed upon is also highly likely to be unhelpful and ineffective as an overall stance and thus the therapist must vary the degree of directiveness according to client characteristics and the stage of therapy. With clients presenting with a high degree of emotional dysregulation and high levels of hostility towards each other during sessions, it may be necessary to be directive in the sense of providing appropriate degrees of structure and acting to divert or interrupt repetitive, unhelpful negative interactions. With clients who show signs of emotional or even physical abusiveness towards their partners, it may be necessary to be highly directive to ensure that such highly negative behaviours are significantly reduced or eliminated. Even as therapy progresses and clients show a greater willingness to experiment with new behaviours as well as a willingness to question or challenge their own cognitions, therapists must be able to 'jump in' at key points to interrupt an interaction that is occurring during the session, asking clients to reflect on what they are aware of happening and directing them to try something different then and there in the session. At the assessment and formulation stages of therapy, the therapist may actively assume a didactive role, providing 'psycho education' regarding the nature of couple distress and skills and strategies of particular relevance to the couple's presenting concerns. As partners move towards being able to use the sessions in a more productive manner and show signs of learning new cognitive and behavioural skills and generalising these to their interactions outside of sessions, the level of directiveness should fade.

In addition to a directive and didactive role, the therapist is required to actively collaborate with clients to find and maintain an appropriate and productive focus for sessions. The therapist ultimately assumes responsibility for managing the pacing and structure of sessions in order to ensure that key therapeutic tasks and interventions are completed in a timely way. Consistent with general practice in CBT, cognitive behavioural couple therapists will be active in working with couples to set an agenda for sessions, to set and review homework assignments and to actively seek feedback, both positive and negative, from clients regarding their experience of specific sessions as well as the therapy overall.

The cognitive behavioural couple therapist also acts as a facilitator during sessions. The aim is to create a good therapeutic alliance with each individual and the couple as a unit. The therapeutic environment is ideally experienced as safe by both partners and in cases where couples initially present with high levels of hostility and negative behaviours, the therapist's ability to be appropriately directive and to interrupt such patterns, and set clear ground rules for maintaining more helpful interaction patterns, is directly related to the establishment and maintenance of a safe and emotionally attuned therapeutic relationship with the couple. In order to facilitate the couple's learning of new skills or embodiment of new standards or beliefs for their relationship, the therapist must skilfully withdraw their use of structure and directiveness in order that the couple begin to generalise these gains to their out-of-session interactions with each other and their environment. The therapist needs to 'keep the ending in mind from the beginning', both in terms of keeping the specific goals (or 'ends') in mind for the intervention (including micro level goals and broader macro level relationship themes) as well as helping the couple to keep in mind those new patterns that they wish to carry forward into their relationship once therapy has ended.

Balance

As has already been implied in the above descriptions concerning flexibility, the therapist also needs to achieve or strive towards balance throughout work with a couple. As was noted earlier, it is important that the therapist strives to achieve a balance of directiveness and collaboration in response to characteristics of the couple and the stage of therapy or the particular therapeutic task being worked with in a session. Across the therapy as a whole the therapist must also strive to balance and integrate cognitive, behavioural emotional and environmentally focussed interventions.

The question of balance is also crucial in terms of the time and attention given to each partner in the relationship. This is important in ensuring that one partner does not experience themselves as having become identified as 'the problem' with an alliance having been formed between the therapist and the other partner. Some couples may be very sensitive to this issue, particularly when they enter therapy with interaction patterns best characterised as expressing 'blaming' of the other as the source of difficulties and an associated hope, stated or unstated, that the therapist will act to 'fix' their errant partner.

Assessment

Assessment in CBCT follows many of the same procedures and principles used in individually focussed CBT and is ongoing throughout therapy. The aims of the assessment stage include:

1. Identifying the nature and extent of the couple's presenting concerns as well as areas of relationship strength and resilience.
2. Understanding the range of cognitive, behavioural, emotional and individual difference factors involved with each partner, the couple relationship and the couple's interactions with their environment.
3. Determining the extent to which CBCT may be an appropriate intervention for these difficulties and the extent to which individual therapy may be necessary as either an alternative or a supplementary intervention to CBCT.

Initial couple interviews

The initial session with a couple can begin by asking each partner for a brief description of the presenting concerns. The therapist can encourage each partner to give a few paragraphs or the 'main headlines' with an acknowledgement that it will be necessary to understand more of the full story as the work unfolds. This emphasis on a brief description allows the therapist to assess the level of agreement between partners around the main issues as well as allowing for an initial assessment of each partner's attributions regarding these problems.

The therapist may then ask the couple to describe the history and development of their relationship. Asking the couple to describe how their relationship first started and how things progressed over time can allow for an in-depth assessment of a wide range of individual, couple and environmental factors. Additionally, as this may require partners to think back to a time when their relationship was likely characterised by more frequent and intense positives, it can challenge the couple to consider the relationship's strengths and positive qualities, that each may be selectively ignoring due to the current level of relationship distress. This description may also aid in understanding each partner's emotional responsiveness and emotional investment in the relationship. For example, an individual who has effectively 'checked out' of the relationship may remain disengaged and flat even when discussing earlier positive times in the relationship.

The discussion of relationship history may then move on to a more in-depth structured assessment of current relationship functioning. This can include an assessment of current environmental demands that are being faced (job stressors, child behaviour problems), resources that the couple has available that are being accessed or are potential resources, and also individual and couple factors that are interfering with the couples' ability to adapt to demands and changes.

Self-report questionnaires

A large number of self-report scales are available for assessing various aspects of individual and relationship functioning. There are no specific scales that are required as part of a CBCT assessment and intervention, and clinical judgement is necessary to decide if the use of a questionnaire will aid in information gathering without overburdening the couple.

Of particular use may be scales that assess each individual's perceptions about the quality of the relationship and the degree of relationship satisfaction they experience. Such scales include the Dyadic Adjustment Scale (DAS; Spanier, 1976) and the Marital Satisfaction Inventory (MSI; Snyder, 1979). These scales allow a broad assessment of various areas of relationship functioning and satisfaction and may be useful also as outcome assessment tools. Ideally, such scales can be completed prior to an initial assessment session with answers to specific items used as a basis for further in-depth discussion in the couple assessment session. Partners need to be informed that responses will be shared during sessions. An important exception to this is the use of scales to assess for the presence of violence and abuse. Often an individual may be unwilling to disclose physical abuse during a couple session due to the reasonable fear that this would provoke further acts of abuse. Scales such as the revised Conflict Tactic Scale (CTS2; Staus et al., 1996) may allow an individual to indicate the presence of abuse to the therapist which must then be carefully assessed in an individual session. Couples can be asked to complete any scales independently and to bring these along to the assessment session. The therapist is then in a position to flexibly assess and discuss various issues that are disclosed through the responses on the questionnaires.

Observation of couple interaction patterns

Whilst couple assessment sessions can be usefully structured to minimise the risk of the couples' interaction becoming unhelpfully 'bogged down', once couples become engaged in discussion of areas of often deep emotional concern the therapist is likely to gain a first-hand observation of typical patterns of interaction and these need to be carefully attended to. The therapist can also ask the couple to engage in a brief interaction task at the end of the couple assessment session in order to allow for a further functional analysis of interaction patterns. Such tasks can focus either on a conversation that involves the expression of thoughts and feelings regarding an issue of moderate concern for the couple or a decision-making conversation again regarding a topic of moderate concern (Baucom and Epstein, 2002). These conversations can either be video recorded and analysed subsequent to the session or the therapist can remain in the session quietly observing the interaction for a 10-minute period. The task of the therapist is to note the relative frequencies of positive and negative interactions and to identify any repetitive patterns such as negative reciprocity and demand-withdraw.

Individual interviews

Individual interviews allow for a more detailed assessment of a range of issues that may affect how each partner functions within the context of an intimate relationship. The range of areas that may be assessed is very wide and ideally the therapist will have entered each individual assessment interview with a range of initial hypotheses derived from the couple assessment interview in order that these can be explored. The individual interview may focus on a more in-depth assessment of individual psychopathology, personality style, as well as the individual's relationship history and family of origin.

During the couple interview the therapist explains the boundaries of confidentiality applicable to the individual assessment interviews. Normally, the discussion that occurs in individual sessions is kept confidential. A number of exceptions exist, however. First, if one partner reveals the presence of an ongoing affair during the individual session then the therapist will wish to work with that individual to determine how they will let their partner know about this. If the individual is unwilling to do so then it may be advisable that the therapist works with that individual towards ending the couple work with a referral for individual sessions, as a couple intervention would not be viable under such circumstances. Another important exception is where one partner reveals the existence of physical abuse. Rather than taking the step of raising this directly in the couple session (which may trigger further instances of violence) the therapist needs to work with the partner who is subject to abuse to look at safety steps, including, for example, moving to a shelter and involving social services in cases where children may be affected. The couple may then be informed that the assessment indicates that couple therapy is not advisable at this stage and that alternative arrangements can be made for individual work.

Feedback and goal setting

Following the completion of the initial assessment, the therapist meets with the couple to give them some feedback about the information that has been gathered and the initial hypotheses about what is maintaining their difficulties. This shared understanding can provide the basis for agreeing an initial plan for therapy.

The therapist aims to provide a relatively 'informal' description of the relationship in terms of its strengths and areas of difficulty and how these are related to various individual, couple interaction and environmental factors. As each partner will often have differing attributions and beliefs about these factors, the therapist strives for a description that does not locate one individual as the source or cause of problems but that also acknowledges that there are important differences in the way each partner understands the situation. Sometimes it will be clear to the therapist that it is indeed the case that issues originating primarily in one of the individuals are having a negative impact on the couple relationship. Where it has been assessed that these individual factors are not best addressed through couple therapy, the therapist can emphasise that the individual is experiencing a range of difficulties that are negatively impacting their ability to address problems within the relationship and that it may be useful for them to address these in individual therapy before coming back to look again at the potential helpfulness of couple therapy.

Epstein and Baucom (2002) recommend that the therapist provides feedback that addresses both macro level themes or patterns as well as micro level behavioural interactions. The therapist can then focus on characteristics of the individuals, the couple and their interactions with the environment that have contributed to the development and maintenance of difficulties as their relationship has developed over time.

DISTINCTIVE PRACTICAL FEATURES OF CBCT

The feedback needs to be presented as part of a dialogue with the couple. Brief descriptions and summaries are provided, with the therapist asking the couple to comment, correct and amend these. The couple may be asked to provide recent illustrative examples of aspects that have been agreed to be of importance and to also indicate other areas of importance that have not yet been adequately described in the therapist's feedback.

An illustrative example of how a feedback session might begin to unfold is presented below:

Therapist: It seems from what you have both told me that at the beginning of your relationship you were both strongly attracted to each other, as you both shared a strong interest in advancing in your separate careers as well as enjoying frequent adventures together on long holidays. You both have strong values around individual achievement as well as the importance of enjoyment and fun. Following the birth of your first son, however, things became much more difficult, partly as a result of the normal challenges of this stage, as well as a result of some of the unpredicted work pressures you were subjected to, Jason. Whilst you both really value having a family, you both talk of how unprepared you were for the changes that this would bring.

This situation has been further complicated by Jason experiencing a period of depression. This has been a real challenge for each of you as you appear to have different styles of communicating around this issue. Jason, you have a tendency to want to retreat and deal with things on your own. Partly this may be an aspect of the depression, and partly this expresses a tendency you describe as always having had. You like to retreat to work on problems in your own head before reaching out to Susan to discuss where you have got to and seeking her support. Susan, you tend to value

	direct communication and problem solving and want to address issues head on. You describe a pattern of approaching Jason to try and resolve things with him getting upset by this and avoiding talking. We talked about how this sort of 'demand-withdraw' cycle is a common and understandable pattern. You also both describe how the overall atmosphere in the relationship has become negative. You are both highly intelligent verbal people and can sometimes use this in ways that express sarcasm and hostility. Does this description ring true for you both?
Jason:	Yes that fits. I really don't feel I have adapted so well to being a parent. I also really don't like it when Susan tries to argue me out of my depression. It just doesn't work.
Therapist:	Yes, we need to look at helping you both find a more effective way of communicating around this issue of your depression, Jason. Susan, how does what I summarised fit for you?
Susan:	It fits pretty well I think. But it hurts hearing what Jason is saying about our family. It's like he doesn't really want us.
Therapist:	It seems to me that each of you has developed some understandable beliefs about why the other is behaving the way that they are. For you, Susan, it seems that Jason's tendency to withdraw and shut down is an expression of him not wanting you or the children. Jason, you have interpreted Susan's anger about your withdrawal as evidence of her not caring. I think an important goal for us to work on is helping you to communicate more effectively around this issue. My sense is that doing so could be useful both in working to reduce Jason's experience of depression and in improving the quality of your relationship. How does that sound in terms of potentially relevant goals for our work?

As illustrated above, this discussion and attempt at a summary may at times result in further expressions of distress that need to be both validated and incorporated into the conceptualisation. The discussion can then continue to specify some provisional goals for the intervention. Ideally, these goals will include both macro level themes such as 'working to regain a sense of connection with each other by spending more time focussed on ourselves as a couple' as well as specific micro level goals such as 'spending at least one night a week on a couple-related activity'.

Closely related to the task of setting reasonable and meaningful treatment goals is contracting for number of sessions. CBCT is a very flexible model that does not specify a particular number of sessions. A typical course of therapy may be between 12 and 18 sessions; however, many couples may require either less or considerably more than this depending upon the nature of their presenting issues. A therapist may choose to contract for an initial 6–8 sessions with the option of reviewing goal attainment and contracting for further sessions.

Behavioural interventions: guided behaviour change

In many instances, behaviour change is a goal in its own right, as increasing the range and frequency of positive behaviours and decreasing the range and frequency of negative behaviours can be a fundamental target of treatment for distressed couples. CBCT also views these behavioural strategies as a highly effective means of working with client's emotions and cognitions and providing a structure within which the couple can address both micro patterns and broader relational themes. Thus, behavioural strategies can often be regarded as the vehicle through which a wide range of issues can be effectively addressed (Epstein and Baucom, 2002).

Epstein and Baucom (2002) classify behavioural strategies into those that involve a skill component and those that do not. Guided behaviour change falls into the latter category in that, in this intervention, the therapist is asking partners to draw upon skills that they already have. Guided behaviour change can be used throughout therapy; however, it is frequently used early on in an effort to make improvements in the overall 'atmosphere' of the relationship. For example, Jason and Susan in the last chapter presented with a pattern of high frequency, but low level, negatives in the form of sarcasm and hostile comments to each other on most days. This had led to a daily experience of the relationship being punishing. Guided behaviour change with this couple might commence with discussions about the usefulness of both partners working to significantly limit the expression of such negatives. Initially this task may be experienced as frustrating as both partners may be experiencing a degree of reward from such negatives (such as a sense of self-righteousness concerning the awfulness of the other partner's behaviour).

Following this, guided behaviour change can be used to increase the frequency of positives. There are many strategies that have been suggested for this, including asking each partner to generate a list of behaviours that they would find rewarding for their partner to enact, with the partner then free to make a choice from amongst these options. Other possibilities include the agreement to hold regular 'couple days' in which the task is for the couple to engage in some form of positive, pleasurable activity together such as going for walks or having a meal out or visiting an art gallery (Fischer et al., 2014).

In previous versions of BCT such positives would be set up in the form of an 'exchange', with one partner agreeing to enact a positive in exchange for some equivalent positive from the other. In contemporary CBCT, this exchange aspect has been de-emphasised. Rather, in a fashion that is resonant with the approach of acceptance and commitment therapy (Hayes et al., 1999) and other third-wave CBT approaches, partners are asked to consider the question of how they would most 'like to be' in regards to their role as a partner. That is, guided behaviour change can be framed in terms of what each individual's values are for how they would like to see themselves behaving in this domain in their life, regardless of their partner's behaviour. Such interventions can be of particular usefulness with couples who report that they have ceased making efforts to express care and concern for each other.

The overarching goal is to help the couple rebuild a pattern of behaviour in which they frequently relate to each other in a caring, respectful, positive manner. There may be an implicit cognitive challenge in such an intervention, as it may be requiring individuals to set aside the potential agenda of 'being right' in the service of finding more functional and rewarding ways of being in the relationship. For some couples the guided behaviour change intervention can also be used in the form of a behavioural 'experiment'. This may be particularly useful in cases where individuals hold beliefs concerning the inability or unwillingness of their partner to engage in any positives at all. It can also be seen that such an overtly behavioural intervention also contains important cognitive components, in that clients' willingness to embark upon this is reliant upon their capacity to self-monitor their own behaviour, to potentially tolerate a degree of discomfort associated from refraining from their regular pattern of negatives and to pay attention to, and track, the positive behaviours displayed by their partner. Thus, whilst this intervention is on the face of it simple and direct, the therapist should pay particular attention to how each partner responds to this – it will provide important information for furthering the assessment. For example, the task of engaging in a 'couple day' or even a 'couple evening' on a regular basis may involve couples making changes to their schedule as well as needing to access resources within the environment, such as extended family for babysitters. The obstacles that they experience here as well as their relative degree of success in negotiating this may disclose relevant information about how the couple relate to their environment and the extent to which they are able to coordinate their actions as a team to do so.

The examples of guided behaviour change interventions provided above are intended to have a fairly broad impact on the overall balance of positive to negatives in a relationship. In addition to these broad changes, guided behaviour change interventions can be more focal and designed to address key relationship themes related to unmet needs and motives. For example, Jason and Susan share strong motives for individual achievement and autonomy. Susan, however, has found herself overwhelmed with tasks related to childcare as well as supporting Jason. An important guided behaviour change intervention may be to work with the couple to rearrange their schedule so that Jason takes a more active role in tasks related to childcare and housework and that Susan has 'protected time' away from home for her to engage in an activity that she finds both meaningful and enjoyable. As well as addressing Susan's need for autonomy, such a task, as a form of behavioural activation, may have a positive impact on Jason's depression. Again, this intervention, although direct and behavioural, may also entail useful cognitive and emotional challenges as well as impacting on the couple's environment. In order to construct focal guided behaviour change interventions that are likely to be meaningful and beneficial, the therapist must have conducted a thorough assessment of the individuals, the couple and their environment.

20

Improving communication: expressive and listening skills

Difficulties in communication are among the most commonly reported problems that couples bring to therapy. Regardless of whether the communication problems are expressive of a long-term skill deficit or whether it is a performance deficit in the current relationship only, the therapist in CBCT will work to establish clear guidelines for good communication within sessions and seek to help couples generalise this to their interactions outside of sessions.

Work on communication skills typically begins with the therapist suggesting that the couple start with conversations that are focussed on sharing thoughts and feelings. Partly, as will be seen in the next chapter, this is because the success of problem-solving conversation also rests on the couple successfully being able to clarify and listen to each other's views about what is important. Additionally, each individual in the couple may need a number of experiences of having been adequately heard and understood by their partner before they are willing to consider problem solving around important issues that affect the relationship.

Sharing thoughts and feelings conversations

Epstein and Baucom (2002) have presented detailed recommendations for therapists to begin the process of helping couples learn principles of clear communication. These principles can be best presented to couples as a series of guidelines which they are encouraged to follow and to explore how they might adopt the 'spirit' of the guidelines into their everyday relationship. It is important to emphasise that these guidelines do not constitute rigid rules for how a couple 'should' communicate. How the couple chooses to take forward the principles into their relationship, given their experience of how these appear to work for them during sessions and during homework tasks, is a topic for respectful exploratory dialogue.

The structure for these conversations emphasises the need for the partners to take up clearly defined roles of 'speaker' and 'listener'. The task, initially, is for the therapist to act as a 'coach', assisting each individual to learn the steps of the process and to stay within the broad guidelines that have been agreed. Couples are asked to choose a topic of moderate emotional intensity in order that a successful experience is more likely and which may allow a sense of competence and confidence to be reinforced. Once the therapist has a sense that the couple has been able to move towards learning (or re-establishing) these skills, the couple is then invited to address more emotionally challenging issues both in the session and during regular, structured practice exercises between sessions.

The guidelines for the speaker and listener roles express the following key principles:

For the speaker

1. Speaking subjectively
   The speaker is encouraged to discuss their experience of the issue in terms of the subjective meanings and emotions that are involved for them. It is important to emphasise that these conversations are not intended to be about establishing 'the truth' about what happened or what is *really* the case.

2. Including emotions
   A common pattern is for individuals to communicate only their thoughts or memories about an issue and to avoid disclosing their emotions about the issue. Where an individual has difficulties in this area, the therapist may need to coach them in identifying and appropriately expressing their key emotions related to an issue.

3. Including the partner
   As a key function of these conversations is facilitating intimacy and connection, the speaker is encouraged to include their feelings about and towards their partner in relation to the issue being addressed.

4. Maintaining balance
   The speaker, who may often be addressing negative events and emotions, is encouraged to also access and include positive emotions they may have towards their partner in what they say. Thus a partner who is angry regarding a forgotten anniversary is also asked to get in touch with and express 'softer' emotions of wanting to feel valued.

5. Appropriate specificity
   In order to avoid overloading the listener with overgeneralised concerns and feelings, the speaker is encouraged to identify and describe their specific emotions and thoughts related to a specific issue.

6. Speaking in paragraphs
   Again, in an effort to increase the likelihood that the listener will be able to take in the communication, the speaker is encouraged to speak in paragraphs rather than presenting a 'novel' so as to allow the listener to deal with one main idea at a time.

7. Using tact and timing
   Here the therapist needs to express that this exercise is not one of 'dumping' on the partner. The task is to find a way of expressing a concern in a manner in which the listener is likely to be able to hear. This includes reflecting upon the best timing and context for holding the conversation. This minimises the possibility of the listener becoming defensive or not being in a position to listen due to it being very late at night or at a

time when they are dealing with competing demands such as children.

For the listener

The skills required for the individual taking up the role of listener are no less challenging for many clients. These include the following:

1. Whilst the speaker is talking, to demonstrate understanding and acceptance of what is being said through tone of voice, facial expressions and other gestures. The key point that may require repeated emphasis is that this acceptance does not equate to agreement. The therapist must work to clarify with couples that it is possible to accept what a partner is saying whilst at the same time maintaining quite a different view on things. Partners are being asked to validate each other's point of view and experience and also express areas where they differ.
2. Whilst the speaker is talking, to attempt to put themselves in the speaker's place. That is, rather than listening primarily from their own point of view, to attempt to tune in to the speaker and gain a good sense of what the experience or concern is like from their perspective.
3. Once the speaker has finished, to attempt to 'give back' what has been heard in terms of a statement or paragraph that captures the speaker's most central emotions, thoughts, dilemmas and concerns. This should not be a simple 'parroting' of what has been said.

In order for the above to be possible, this role also requires the listener to avoid the following:

1. Interrupting frequently with questions or alternative perspectives or solutions.
2. Statements that are more of an interpretation of what the listener thinks the speaker *really* means.
3. Statements that express a judgement or rejection of what the speaker has said.

Therapists will often find that many sessions may be focussed on assisting couples to work within these guidelines. Having done so to a reasonable degree, the couple's willingness to work with each other in this manner also provides the necessary structure for them to address issues related to both primary and secondary sources of distress.

Improving communication: decision-making conversations

In order for a couple to function well as a team, they need to be able to hold conversations that are focussed on making decisions and solving problems. A very wide range of issues may fall under the category of problem-solving conversations such as finances, household chores, holiday plans, ways that leisure time is used and issues around bringing up children.

Many factors can work to make such conversations difficult or ineffective. For example, a demand-withdraw pattern may be in operation, with the withdrawing partner refusing to engage in conversations on topics in which they wish to maintain the status quo. Alternatively, once conversations begin, either one or both partners may find it difficult to stay focussed upon a specific topic and the conversation moves so broadly that no outcomes are produced. Conversations can also break down due to expressions of hostility and blaming which results in one or both partners withdrawing from the effort at problem solving.

The following set of guidelines require partners to demonstrate a willingness to continue with the model of 'turn taking' and accurate and respectful listening and expression that has been worked with in the sharing thoughts and feelings exercise. A description of these guidelines, elaborated more fully in Epstein and Baucom (2002), is as follows:

1. Each partner is invited to state the issue or problem in clear, specific and non-blaming terms and the partners are asked to agree on a problem statement as the basis for further discussion.

Many of the difficulties that occur for couples in holding decision-making conversations occur at this first stage. Couples are encouraged to co-construct a statement that focusses on a present concern rather than an overgeneralised statement that includes a great deal of historical reference. Thus, 'We need to find a solution for your lifelong laziness and unwillingness to be involved with the children as a good parent should be' is an unworkable statement for several obvious reasons. Couples may initially present a statement that covers a complex range of issues that need to be broken down and dealt with in stages. The problem statement also needs to be primarily a description of an issue rather than already a statement of a preferred outcome, as in the example above. The statement 'I would like to discuss how we have divided tasks related to the care of our children' is a more workable statement. As in the sharing thoughts and feelings exercise, the request that the couple agree on a statement does not constitute a suggestion that they think about, feel or see the issue in the same terms. One partner may in fact not see the issue as something that needs change; however, their willingness to engage with their partner in an area of concern that is meaningful to them is likely to be a positive step for the relationship.

2. Each partner is invited to state why the issue is important for them and what it is they want or desire.

This step is clearly reliant upon the partners' skills in sharing thoughts and feelings. The guideline asks partners to work together to clarify the underlying meaning of the problem and what a solution needs to address. Thus, a conversation that is at one level about the division of household chores also becomes a conversation about the importance one of both partners places on the values of 'equality' and 'respect'. It is important that this step is not rushed as there may be a number of important meanings that are associated with issues that on the surface appear very 'day to day'.

3. Partners are invited to propose and discuss potential solutions.

Rather than simply state a solution that is in keeping with the individual's preferences, partners are invited to suggest solutions that embody the important meanings and needs of both individuals. This step is likely to be quite novel for many couples, particularly where their default style is a struggle over competing solutions, with one partner 'winning' and another 'losing' or giving in.

4. Partners are invited to decide upon a solution 'for now'.

Rather than suggesting the couple makes a once-and-for-all decision, many issues allow for the couple to agree on an initial proposal that can be tried out and reviewed after a set time frame. The time frame can be negotiated with a further agreement to review how the potential solution has worked for each individual and the couple.

There are some decisions, however, such as whether or not to have a child, where no such 'provisional solution' is possible and where each partner may maintain a dichotomous position. In such situations Epstein and Baucom (2002) suggest discussing with each partner whether they feel it is likely that they will be successful in changing their partner's mind. Where partners are able to recognise that such a change of mind is unlikely, the therapist can encourage the couple to remain with the task of exploring the various meanings, values and emotions that are contained in this issue. Such an exploration may also involve the couple confronting the necessity of one of the partners making the decision to put their partner's needs and desires first in order for it to be possible to go forward, without the act of doing so being done as a form of self-sacrifice that will later breed resentment and anger.

As may be clear in the above discussion as well as the last chapter, the work on communication skills involves the therapist being able to focus upon both the process of communication as well as the content. In terms of process, the therapist is aiming to establish and shape workable patterns of communication that will be maintained after the couple ends therapy. In terms of content, the therapist needs to be able to flexibly work with the couple during these structured interventions to address key areas that will be related to broad relationship themes. The therapist does not make the assumption that if the couple can simply be taught to communicate appropriately then their issues will be resolved. Whilst improving communication between partners is likely to improve the quality of the relationship in many respects, this is of course not guaranteed. A couple may successfully clarify and understand each other's respective needs around autonomy versus togetherness, for example, but this does not ensure that they will successfully be able to come to a workable compromise around significant differences between them in the level of these respective needs. Good communication around such issues is essential, however, to allow for the possibility of such negotiation and reorganisation to occur.

Challenging cognitions: selective attention and attributions

A central aim of the therapist in CBCT is to assist the partners to become aware of their cognitive content and process, to be more able to gain some experiential distance from this, as well as to challenge unhelpful cognitions and construct and test out new, more functional cognitions. Many of the strategies used in individual forms of CBT such as thought diaries and behavioural experiments can also be employed within the context of couple therapy. There are a number of modifications, however, that need to be made due to the nature of the context for couple therapy.

In individual CBT, a therapist may assist a client to identify distorted cognitions and to understand and label the nature of these distortions. This can include, for example, identifying instances of 'catastrophising' (you forgot my birthday, this must mean you are having an affair and are going to leave me), 'dichotomous thinking' (you either support every decision I make or it means you have no respect for me), and 'selective attention' (all you do is criticise me, I hear nothing else from you). The therapist is likely to then utilise a strategy of 'Socratic Dialogue' (Beck, 1996) in which a series of questions are asked, directing the client to examine the logic of their thinking as well as its evidential basis. Clients may be asked, for instance, if they can think of any evidence from their own experience that contradicts or is not consistent with their thoughts. This then provides a basis for greater flexibility and the construction of new, more helpful cognitions that can then be reinforced or modified further through behavioural and other strategies. Such strategies can be very effective in the context of individual therapy, where the therapist has successfully established a strong therapeutic relationship and an atmosphere of trust and openness. In the context of couple therapy, however, the individual is often not only in the presence of a supportive therapist but also their partner, who may at times be expressing hostility as well as direct challenges to the way they are thinking about the relationship. Thus, therapeutic strategies such as Socratic Dialogue that present direct challenges to cognitions may often be ineffective and counter-productive. Partners are more likely to respond with defensiveness when challenged directly, and this also runs the risk of having an individual 'lose face' in front of their partner and experience the therapist as having formed an alliance with their partner against them.

The therapist may need to proceed carefully and flexibly in challenging cognitions in couple sessions. There are a range of strategies that the therapist can employ to assist partners to identify, monitor and challenge their attributions and patterns of selective attention. First, the therapist needs to be sufficiently attuned to the client's cognitions and adept at asking a client to slow down and to report on what cognitions they are experiencing, and the meanings implicit in these. The therapist can also present 'mini talks' on the important role of cognitions without locating the problem as existing with either individual. Couples can be asked to become aware of their 'self-talk' about themselves, their partner and the relationship and to hold to the possibility that some of these cognitions may be accurate, some may be distorted and some may be unhelpful. Partners should be informed that it would be definitely unhelpful in most instances for them to attempt to challenge the cognitions of their partner!

Epstein and Baucom (2002) argue that in contrast to the use of Socratic dialogue, strategies of 'guided discovery' are far more likely to be effective in couple therapy. Rather than focussing on a direct, primarily rational-logical challenge of a client's cognitions, guided discovery interventions involve creating new experiences. Where such experiences can be created, the therapist is then able to direct the client's attention to aspects of this which will, in turn, allow the client to challenge their own cognitions and to develop new cognitions without triggering defensiveness or shame and without the risk of exposing them to criticisms from their partner to the effect of 'see, I always told you that you were thinking crazy!'

Many guided discovery interventions can be incorporated into the behavioural interventions that have been described in previous chapters, such as guided behaviour change and communication exercises. For example, a client may present with a key cognition 'my partner never listens to me because he is uncaring'. It is possible that this cognition is an expression of both selective attention (the partner is only processing those instances where her partner appears not to listen) as well as an attribution (the behaviour of 'not listening' is attributed to an internal, stable, global and negative trait of being 'uncaring'). Challenged directly on this cognition, the client is likely to respond with a great deal of evidence as to why this cognition is accurate. An alternative strategy is to assist the couple to learn and work with the sharing thoughts and feelings exercise. To the degree that the therapist is successful in helping the couple learn these skills, the individual will have an experience of their partner attending to what they are saying, refraining from interrupting and attempting to summarise and feed back important meanings and emotions. As part of this exercise the therapist is then able to ask the individual to reflect, for example:

T: Mary, what was it like for you to see Greg work hard to try and listen well to what you were saying, even though he does see things in a very different way?

M: Well, he did seem to listen, I know he doesn't agree but at least he seemed willing to try and understand. That does at least make me feel more hopeful.

As can be seen in this hypothetical example, some cognitive dissonance has been produced and a degree of willingness to consider an alternative cognition. The client has by no means simply modified the cognition in a way that will maintain over time. Further negative behavioural interactions are likely to lead to a re-triggering of the original cognition. Ideally, the therapist will also have noted that the cognition 'you don't listen to me' is a key cross-situational, or 'macro level' theme that is related to unmet relational needs. This will support the therapist in regularly checking out the strength of the client's belief in this key cognition as the couple attempt to conduct couple conversations between sessions as well as introduce other behavioural changes.

Challenging cognitions: relationship standards and beliefs

Working with cognitions in most forms of CBT typically commences with relatively surface level automatic thoughts and patterns of distorted thinking and then moves on to clarifying and modifying 'deeper' cognitions such as assumptions and 'rules for living' (Leahy, 1997). Similarly, in CBCT the therapist works to help partners clarify their assumptions about relationships and their expectations and standards for how they believe their relationships 'should' be. These deeper forms of cognition can also be regarded as 'broader' as they are active across many different situations and may reflect important macro level themes in the relationship. A commonly used technique in individual CBT is the 'Downward Arrow' which can help a therapist clarify the implicit meanings in a relatively surface level cognition that is associated with strong emotion (Beck, 1996). This strategy can be employed in CBCT to help clarify important relational standards and beliefs. An example of how this might work with Mary and Greg from the previous chapter is as follows:

T: Mary, you have spoken a number of times about how upset you feel when your sense is that Greg is not as available to you as you would like him to be. This sounds like an important area for us to understand further. Would you be willing to look at this? What does it mean to you when you think he is not available?

M: It means he doesn't care. It's like he's not interested.

G: But I do care! And we do spend time together. It's like you are saying I completely ignore you or something!

M: I know you are trying but it shouldn't be so hard. I mean, your partner should always be available to you, no matter what!

T: So, Mary, for you this sounds like an important standard you hold. We all hold standards or beliefs about how we think our relationships should be like. How would you put that? If it was like a kind of general rule . . . in a good relationship . . .

M: We should always be available to each other no matter what else is happening. We should be available for each other 100 per cent of the time.

Having clarified an important relationship standard, this information can be used to enrich the conceptualisation of the couples presenting difficulties. Further work may clarify that the couple have quite different standards for this area of functioning. Such standards need to be explored carefully and respectfully as they are likely to be expressive of a wide range of factors. Relationship standards may in part reflect important cultural beliefs regarding gender roles or how power can and should be expressed in relationships. Relationship standards are also likely to be expressive of the individual's developmental history and family of origin. Such standards, although at times appearing extreme, or from the therapist's point of view, distorted or unhelpful, are also primarily functional in that they help individuals make sense of events in their relationship. As Epstein and Baucom (2002) argue, helping couples clarify and modify their relationship standards is best done by examining how particular standards function rather than challenging them through an appeal to rationality. That is, cognitions at the level of general rules for how things should be are best challenged through interventions that help partners explore the positive and negative consequences of current standards as well as exploring the potential positive and negatives associated with any considered modification to current standards.

Epstein and Baucom (2002) have outlined a series of steps that the therapist can guide the couple in engaging with, in an intervention designed to help couples to explore current standards and to co-construct new standards when this seems desirable or appropriate. The therapist will likely introduce this intervention after some time has been devoted to exploring each partner's standards. Thus for Mary the expectation may be clarified 'We should always be available to each other no matter what else is going on.' Whilst for Greg there is an alternative expectation of 'We need to give each other as much space as needed. Togetherness is important but private space and time alone is more important.' This difference may also have been explored in terms of the partner's respective differences in needs for autonomy versus needs for togetherness. It could be argued further that this expresses a couple level 'existential tension' in which the couple have become polarised. In working to co-construct a standard or expectation that may be expressive of both partners' needs and 'owned position' on this polarity or tension, the therapist may help the couple to:

1. Clarify each person's standard as a clear statement of belief.
2. Ask the partners to list the advantages and disadvantages of each person's standard. This can often best be done by asking one partner to start listing the advantages of the other person's standard rather than just speaking from their own position.
3. Explore areas of possible overlap and work to co-construct a potential common standard that may maximise the advantages and minimise the disadvantages for both partners. This should be a standard that includes the important values and needs of both individuals.
4. Operationalise this potential new standard into specific behaviours for each person.
5. Ask the couple to experiment with the new behaviours and the new standard for a trial period.
6. In subsequent sessions, work on problem solving difficulties that arise in the trial period, emphasising that deeper level cognitions such as standards do not shift quickly.
7. Work with the couple to modify the new standard in the light of new experience and to make it more workable or flexible as needed.

Couples can often struggle to change deeply held, long-term standards for relationships and it is important not to give the impression that there is an expectation that they will simply be able to drop an old standard that is possibly expressive of important values and take up a new standard. Prepared in this way, couples are more able to work with apparent setbacks and unanticipated obstacles. At other times, couples may find that they are unable to reach an agreement on a potential new standard. This may be due to having very different personality traits and motives along the dimension that the standards relate to. In these circumstances, the therapist can work with the couple to clarify and make sense of this difference as well as explore the extent to which it will be possible for each of them to accept and live with these differences without further attempt to change the other, and what potential consequences there are for the relationship and for them as individuals if they are unable to accept these differences (Fischer et al., 2014).

# 24

Working with emotions

Couples can present with a wide variety of difficulties in the emotional domain. These can range from couples where one or both partners show difficulties in accessing and expressing emotions, to those couples where one or both partners present with difficulties in containing the experience or expression of emotion. Equally, couples may present with one partner who struggles with a restricted emotional range whilst their partner struggles with difficulties in containing and appropriately expressing intense emotions. The couple therapist needs to carefully assess and understand the range of difficulties that each partner experiences in this domain and how these interact in order to select appropriate interventions.

Strategies for working with restricted emotional experience and expression

A number of strategies from emotion-focussed therapy (Johnson, 2004) can be adopted in order to work with couples where one or both partners have difficulties in accessing, experiencing, describing and/or expressing emotions. All of these strategies rely upon the therapist's ability to have co-constructed a safe and trusting therapeutic relationship. Where a good enough relationship has been established, the therapist is then able, initially through brief psycho-educational mini talks, to address the importance of emotion in couple functioning and the value of emotional expression.

Whilst emotional experience can be focussed upon at any point in a session, often this domain can be usefully addressed during structured communication exercises such as the sharing thoughts and feeling exercise. It is often the case that during the initial stages of working with this, the therapist will note that one or both partners struggles with accessing, experiencing and/or expressing their emotions. Initially a therapist, in their role as 'coach' during such exercises, can interrupt the conversation in order to direct an individual to pause and to attempt to focus more clearly on their emotion. In doing so, the therapist can carefully use their 'self' including posture, tone of voice and pace of speech to help the individual to access their emotions. On many occasions, such interventions are sufficient to support an individual who is struggling with a degree of experiential avoidance of their emotions. At other times, such encouragement from the therapist will reveal that the client continues to struggle with this. The therapist then has a range of options including the use of metaphors and images, asking the client to recount emotional experiences and asking the client to add additional description to moments of key emotions. The therapist can also question the client about their physiological sensations associated with moments where emotions would be expected to have arisen. The therapist may also use reflections and questions designed to assist the individual to 'stay with' their emotional experience long enough so that it takes shape and that it becomes more possible for them to give a description of this. For clients that struggle finding appropriate language for their emotions, the therapist can provide a list of different emotion words or images to help them develop a richer emotional language. As the individual begins to access and express their emotions, it then becomes important for the therapist to ensure that their partner accurately listens and responds to the emotions that are communicated. The sharing thoughts and feelings exercise then becomes a vehicle in which both partners shape up and positively reinforce each other's functional expression of emotion.

At the same time, the therapist needs to have assessed for the presence of culturally based norms and beliefs regarding this domain rather than assuming a western 'therapeutic ideology' that equates health with a high degree of emotional expressiveness (Fischer et al., 2014). Additionally, the therapist also needs to have assessed for the role of normal individual differences, such as introversion-extraversion, that will likely influence the degree to which an individual is comfortable with work in this domain and the likely limitations placed on change in this area.

Strategies for helping clients contain the experience and expression of emotion

Clients often present in couple therapy with difficulties containing negative emotion. This is a frequent feature of couple distress and it is important for the therapist to assess for the degree to which the apparent difficulties in the areas of emotional regulation and expression are a feature primarily of the current couple distress, or are expressive of long-term, cross-situational difficulties for one or both of the partners. There are a range of cognitive and behavioural strategies that can assist individuals to more effectively moderate their experience and expression of emotion. Such strategies include those that target cognition, such as helping clients identify and challenge beliefs they hold about the need to strongly express all their negative emotions. Additionally, the therapist can use strategies that more directly target the client's experience and expression of strong emotion. For example, the therapist can work to help partners to structure their time so that secure and reliable space becomes available for partners to express emotions. This works against a tendency for one or both partners to express strong emotions in inappropriate contexts, due to a fear that their emotions and needs will not be addressed if they do not express these immediately. Similarly, during communication exercises the therapist can coach the partners in moderating their intensity of emotional expression and again ensuring that such changes are reinforced by their partner's greater willingness to listen and respond to more moderated expressions of emotion.

Some individuals may present in couple therapy with longer-term difficulties in emotional regulation. Such individuals may struggle with the communication exercises as described in this text. Recently, Kirby and Baucom (2007) have described the integration of principles and strategies from dialectical behaviour therapy (DBT) to assist such individuals. Interventions from DBT can be used to improve an individual's ability to tolerate distress. Strategies that help individuals 'self-sooth' and become mindfully aware of their experience, as well as 'response delay' strategies that encourage individuals to delay immediately expressing strong negative feelings, can be of great benefit when these strategies are incorporated into an interpersonal perspective. Where one or both partners show clear deficits in emotional regulation skills it may also be advisable for the therapist to see each partner for a series of individual sessions in order to more effectively coach them in these skills. Alternatively, if the emotional dysregulation difficulties are too severe to be addressed in couple therapy, and particularly where such difficulties exist alongside forms of partner abuse, the therapist may refer one or both of the partners for an individual intervention, with the couple therapy being resumed at a later date.

Working with the environment

CBCT requires therapists to maintain an essentially systemic understanding of the role of the environment in the genesis and maintenance of couple distress. Epstein and Baucom (2002) emphasise that the environment can be understood in terms of 'layers' of factors including the physical, interpersonal, familial, social and cultural environment. Additionally, couples may be affected not only by the current environment but also by what they have each carried forward in terms of their learning history in previous environments. Earlier in this book I have suggested that the metaphor of a 'horizon' can usefully express the effect of context in both providing possibilities and resources for action and the co-creation of meaning as well as placing limitations on these.

Couples frequently present in therapy either underestimating or overestimating the role of environmental factors in their current difficulties. For example, Shamina and Sandeep present with a high degree of negative reciprocity and significant areas of difference in terms of expectations and beliefs about parenting. They both tend to blame each other for these 'faults' as well as themselves for being seemingly unable to resolve their problems. Assessment reveals that the couple are from different ethnic-religious groups where, historically, both groups have been highly disapproving of intermarriage. Shamina and Sandeep report that they had both lost contact with their parents and wider family systems as a result of going ahead with their relationship. This status as 'outcasts' has been softened by the arrival of their two children, and both their mothers have reinitiated contact. However, there remain significant tensions and hostility within the wider system.

In working with such a couple, the role of the environment should be taken into account at all stages of the intervention. First, in the assessment and feedback sessions the therapist can outline how, in their view, the level of demand placed upon the couple by this wider systemic issue has greatly impacted on their coping resources. The couple, both of whom were educated in Europe and attained higher academic degrees, maintained beliefs that they should be able to 'go it alone' and that any attempt to seek support for their families would be tantamount to admitting failure. The therapist needs to validate both the partners' high degree of resilience whilst also working to acknowledge the very real effect on the couple of this complex interpersonal environment. There may be options, however, for the couple to be assisted to explore how to use the environment more effectively to meet their needs.

CBCT includes a wide range of interventions that can assist couples in responding to environmental demands as well as making best use of available environmental resources. Problem-solving skills have long been used within BCT as a method of assisting couples in responding more effectively to the environment. Thus, Shamina and Sandeep, who have both been very stressed by the demands of caring for their two children whilst both maintain jobs in academia, may benefit from problem-solving and decision-making conversations around topics such as accessing appropriate childcare from their extended family in a way that minimises conflict with family members that continue to regard them as outcasts. Inevitably, this will also involve work with each partner's cognitions and emotions surrounding this difficult systemic issue. Additionally, it may be revealed that past aspects of the partners' environments continue to exert influence. Shamina grew up in an environment where a high degree of deference was shown to male members of the family, and losing contact with her extended family has been particularly hard on her as she has experienced both her own and her partner's family as attributing the blame for their going ahead with the relationship to her 'poor moral character' and 'selfish scheming'. She may have beliefs that she is ultimately more to blame for their problems and therefore not deserving of help. She may also believe she should be totally responsible for childcare despite her own demanding job and her motives for individual achievement. Communication work may be useful in helping the couple to understand the effect of this past environment and its relationship to expectations and beliefs that are functioning to make it even more difficult for the couple to adapt to the current environment.

Additionally, work on the couple's expectations could be useful as it may be revealed that the substantial degree of inequality that exists in the current relationship, particularly as is expressed in beliefs about how housework and finances should be managed, are adding additional sources of stress as well as a disproportionate burden on Shamina. Work on the issues of power and equality in the relationship may be challenging. The therapist needs to be sensitive both to validate the couple's beliefs that their respective upbringing has led them to conclude that an unequal distribution of power is inevitable and appropriate, whilst at the same time helping them to explore the advantages and disadvantages of running their current relationship in a manner consistent with these beliefs versus choosing to explore alternative relational expectations that allow for a greater degree of equality and flexibility. The fact that the couple have a history of successfully challenging culturally based beliefs may be used as a resource to help them explore possible changes in this domain as well.

Additional interventions may also help a couple access more effectively available environmental resources. For example, Shamina and Sandeep may need to access sources of support outside of their respective families and may also benefit from interventions aimed at helping them learn more effective parenting skills. Such interventions may include psychoeducation and informational presentations, guided behaviour change and behavioural experiments where acting on these suggestions also involves challenging important beliefs and expectations.

Sequencing interventions

It will be recalled from chapter one that CBCT proposes that couple distress can be usefully understood and addressed at two levels:

1. Primary distress: the distress that arises where partners are unable to successfully resolve issues that can be traced to their patterns of similarity and difference in terms of basic needs and motives.
2. Secondary distress: the distress which develops as a consequence of the couple's ineffective interactions, which are expressions of their efforts at coping with and resolving primary distress.

The distinction between primary and secondary distress is very useful clinically as it allows for a comprehensive formulation and treatment plan. Most usually, initial interventions in CBCT target secondary distress. However, couples need to be assured that primary distress will become an explicit focus of the work and may be reluctant to consider altering behaviour and cognitions that maintain secondary distress, unless their concerns around not having important needs met in the relationship is addressed by the therapist. In responding to such concerns, the therapist can validate partners' anxieties and the fact that the secondary distress that they are experiencing is expressive of their best efforts at solving the sources of primary distress. As therapy proceeds, the therapist may find that the work oscillates between interventions targeting secondary distress and work that addresses primary distress. A couple that succeeds in reducing unhelpful patterns of interaction in order to provide a platform for addressing primary areas of difficulty may find themselves reverting to 'old ways' as the work progresses and touches upon often complex and difficult issues that may trigger strong emotions.

DISTINCTIVE PRACTICAL FEATURES OF CBCT

Interventions targeting secondary distress

Previous chapters have described a wide range of interventions that can be used to target secondary distress. These include interventions to modify behaviour such as guided behaviour change and skill-based interventions that seek to help couples learn effective means for expressive communication and accurate listening. Additionally, interventions can directly target cognitive aspects of secondary distress by helping couples learn to identify and challenge patterns of selective attention and attributions as well as underlying cognitions expressive of relational assumptions and standards. Emotional interventions may also be incorporated to help couples learn to more effectively experience, regulate and express their emotional experience. These interventions need to be sequenced in a flexible manner that allows a balance of attention on cognitive, emotional and behavioural domains. According to Epstein and Baucom (2002), in choosing interventions, the therapist seeks to aid couples in reducing secondary distress by:

1. Increasing each partner's ability to notice the existence of the pattern and to improve their ability to engage in relational, circular thinking (relational schematic processing).
2. Decrease the frequency of partners relying on overlearned behaviours from previous relationships. This may include, for example, helping couples identify how patterns of hostility, learnt in prior relationships, are maintained in the present one due to them being at least partly effective in getting some needs met, or resulting in a cessation of aversive interactions. Guided behaviour change and skills-based interventions may be used to achieve reductions in the frequency and intensity of these behaviours as well as helping to substitute more functional positive behaviour patterns.
3. Establishing and maintaining clear guidelines for couple interaction inside and outside of sessions.
4. Altering partners' cognitions about each other's behaviour.
5. Improving emotional regulation and expression.

As the therapist works to help the couple identify the patterns that maintain the secondary distress, it is also important that the therapist helps to clarify how this is expressive of important underlying issues that have yet to be resolved.

Interventions for resolving primary relationship issues and dilemmas

Once secondary distress has been reduced, many of the cognitive, behavioural, affective and environmental interventions can then be flexibly used to target primary sources of distress. The major aims of interventions that target primary distress, according to Epstein and Baucom (2002), include:

1. Helping partners improve their awareness of each other's needs, motives and personality styles and the extent to which they have been able to find ways to address these in their relationship.
2. Working to increase partners' acceptance of their individual differences rather than viewing these as sources of inevitable conflict or attributing these to flaws in their partner's character.
3. Increasing partners' self-efficacy and ability to make changes aimed at reconciling areas of significant difference.

As Jacobson and Christensen (1996) note, a key target for intervention can often involve helping partners step away from efforts at changing their partner and embracing the possibility of accepting areas of difference. Such efforts are by no means easy or straightforward and may often involve difficult challenges for couples in terms of their basic beliefs and desires.

Many of the interventions which are used initially to reduce secondary distress can be used in a flexible manner to help target primary distress. For example, a couple may have worked to reduce a pattern of demand-withdraw which has also helped identify that each of them differs substantially in needs for intimacy versus needs for autonomy. Following this, the therapist may use a variety of strategies including psychoeducation to normalise these differences. Work on each partner's attributions may help the partners to revise their understanding of the reasons for their partner's behaviour. In moving on to address this source of primary distress, the therapist can then continue to use the communication skills as an effective vehicle for the work that allows for cognitive, affective, behavioural and environmental aspects to be addressed. By staying with the communication guidelines, partners may gain a more nuanced and complex understanding of each other's motives and needs and often experience a softening of their attributions, assumptions and standards for how their relationship should work. The therapist can also guide the couple in exploring potential new beliefs and standards that may allow for a better accommodation of each partner's needs and preferences. Behavioural experiments and other homework assignments can be co-constructed to allow possible new ways of relating to be 'road tested'. Again, such work is often complex and challenging for the therapist and the couple as they consider the extent to which it is possible for them to evolve more satisfying patterns within the limitations imposed by their respective temperaments, learning histories, beliefs and current resources and demands.

Addressing individual psychopathology: the case of depression

Baucom et al. (1998) outline three types of couple-based interventions that can be used when psychopathology is present in one or both partners:

1. partner-assisted interventions
2. disorder-specific couple interventions
3. formal couple therapy.

In practice these three categories may significantly overlap. This chapter considers how these forms of intervention might be used in the very frequently encountered example where one or both partners presents with depression.

Partner-assisted interventions

In partner-assisted interventions one partner is asked to act as a surrogate therapist or coach in assisting the 'identified patient' to address their individual psychopathology. In the case of depression, interventions involving behavioural activation can be particularly helpful and the therapist can employ guided behaviour change to assist the couple in carrying out this intervention. Providing the non-depressed partner with information about depression, and a rationale for interventions, can also work to alter unhelpful attributions regarding the depressed partner's behaviour and support the non-depressed partner in providing social support.

One issue that often needs to be addressed in cases of depression is risk of suicide. On occasion it may be very important to work with both partners on steps the non-depressed partner can take if they become concerned that the risk for self-harm is becoming greater. An agreed action plan, in which the non-depressed partner has been empowered to act in the best interests of the individual and the relationship, even in the face of the depressed partner's disagreement that action is appropriate, can be a necessary clinical intervention. Such an intervention is likely to be facilitated by psychoeducation as well as work on communication.

As Epstein and Baucom (2002) note, such interventions often can't be regarded as having a neutral effect on the relationship, as it is possible that by asking one partner to take on the role of surrogate therapist, the balance of power within the relationship will be challenged in some fashion. The therapist needs to have carefully assessed the likely impact of such interventions, otherwise non-compliance or resistance from one of both partners is more likely. However, when a partner can be engaged in this fashion, doing so may greatly facilitate the co-construction of various exposure tasks that can be useful in a variety of clinical presentations.

Disorder-specific couple interventions

This class of interventions focusses on the relationship and in particular the manner in which the couple's interactions patterns have contributed to the triggering and maintenance of the individual's depression. Additionally, these interventions focus on clarifying how the individual's difficulties have impacted on the relationship and attempt to ameliorate this impact. For our couple Jason and Susan (Chapter 13), many appropriate CBCT interventions would fit into this category. This is due to the extent to which Susan has been negatively impacted by Jason's experience of depression, both directly in terms of the impact on relationship distress and indirectly as her efforts at supporting him have functioned to lessen the extent to which she is able to have some of her own individually oriented needs met both inside and outside of the relationship. Below are some examples of disorder-specific couple interventions that could be helpful in this case example:

THE CASE OF DEPRESSION

- Guided behaviour change to reduce the frequency and intensity of negative behaviours from both partners. Reducing negative reciprocity may be helpful for couple distress and may remove one factor that may be functioning as a maintenance factor for individual depression.
- Behavioural activation: the couple can be assisted to engage in behavioural activation both as a couple and as individuals. This may enable the couple to make more effective contact with their environment. The goal is to increase positive behaviours focussed on the couple as well as positive behaviours for each individual; to reduce Jason's symptoms of depression and also to allow Susan to begin to meet some of her individually oriented needs.
- Communication training: the couple can be assisted to learn expressive and listening skills. Such conversations may have each individual's experience of the depression as their focus.
- Work on emotions: within the context of communications interventions, Jason may be assisted to get in contact with and to express a wider range of emotions. Additionally, Susan may also be encouraged to express a wider range of emotions, including appropriate anger and sadness about the extent to which Jason's depression has impacted her and their children. This may connect to some cognitive work as Susan may have avoided such emotional expressions due to an understandable expectation that doing so will be responded to negatively by Jason. Jason, who has spent a large amount of time expressing negative affect, may also be coached to use appropriate 'compartmentalisation' to ensure that the couple has time where 'the depression' is not the main focus of attention.
- Work on cognitions: a clear maintaining factor for Jason's depression may be a high degree of negative automatic thoughts that he is often expressing to Susan. It would be inappropriate to ask Susan to act as Jason's cognitive therapist. It would also likely be ineffective as Jason is not likely to respond well to Susan's attempts at challenging his cognitions. Instead, the couple can be coached in how to provide appropriate and helpful

statements of social support that reinforce Susan's belief that Jason is capable of overcoming his difficulties whilst also validating the fact that he is currently experiencing distress. Sessions can include role-play practice of these sorts of interactions. The possibility of 'role-reversal' exercises could also be incorporated here, which may help both partners gain a more complete understanding of how each experiences their interactions.

Formal couple therapy

The interventions as described above may naturally evolve into more formal couple therapy. Jason entered this relationship with a vulnerability to depression and it was clarified that this more recent triggering of his depression was related to the couple entering into the normal developmental stage of having children and experiencing an adjustment of their respective roles. The couple may be assisted to understand more clearly what each has brought forward into this relationship in terms of their basic needs and motivations. The fact that the relationship has run into trouble at this stage, where it has become practically more difficult for each partner to meet their needs, can be considered as a helpful aspect of an overall formulation. The couple can be assisted to engage in problem-solving conversations that can focus on how to more effectively work as a team to ensure that the needs of both partners are met in the relationship (particularly as Jason's symptoms of depression start to improve and his ability to provide both instrumental and social support to Susan contributes to a growing sense of self efficacy). Additionally, the couple's expectations and beliefs about how their relationship 'should' function can be explored and negotiated as this relates to issues such as equality and power in the relationship. Both couple sessions and individual sessions may be helpful for exploring family-of-origin issues and how these have been carried forward and have influenced how each partner has responded to Jason's experience of depression and his likely ongoing vulnerability to this in the future.

Infidelity and relational trauma

Couples presenting with issues surrounding infidelity are amongst the presentations that clinicians from all orientations frequently experience as the most difficult to manage (Whisman et al., 1997). At the same time, infidelity is a common trigger for seeking the services of a couple therapist, with studies suggesting that 30 per cent of couples seek therapy due to an infidelity (Whisman et al., 1997). Gordon et al. (2008) have argued that infidelity, along with a range of other events such as partner physical and/or emotional abuse, can be regarded as a form of 'interpersonal trauma' and have presented a model to help clinicians work with such couples. The model integrates concepts and strategies from CBCT and IOCT and draws upon models of post-traumatic stress and research on forgiveness.

Shattered assumptions

The literature on traumatic reactions suggests that events that are experienced as traumatic may have their impact via a shattering of the individual's assumptions about who they are and the way the world works. With infidelity, the 'injured party' can be understood as struggling to make sense of the meaning of the infidelity as this may have shattered their assumptions of 'belonging' and 'safety' with their partner. At the same time the 'participating partner' may also be struggling with their own emotions of guilt and depression at having behaved in a fashion that may be inconsistent with their values. They may also be struggling with unresolved emotions regarding the affair partner as well as possible feelings of loss regarding that relationship, if it has ended.

The model suggests that the work can be understood as progressing in the following stages: (1) 'absorbing the blow', (2) 'gaining understanding' and (3) 'moving forward'. Each stage is understood as involving a number of tasks which will often involve strong emotional, cognitive and behavioural reactions that will need to be addressed.

Absorbing the blow

In the initial stages, particularly if the couple have commenced therapy shortly after the discovery of an infidelity, the injured party may describe being emotionally overwhelmed and struggling to regulate their emotions and behaviour. They may experience their partner and their life as unpredictable and unsafe. There is also a risk of the injured party acting to seek 'revenge' or restitution against their partner and/or the third party through destructive behaviours.

Establishing clear boundaries, in an effort to provide safety and containment for both partners, is essential. This may involve reaching agreements regarding the degree of contact that the participating partner has with the third party. This may be complex and difficult work where there is an ongoing affair that the participating partner is ambivalent about ending. The therapist can use strategies of psychoeducation and guided behaviour change to clarify 'rules for engagement', including time-out periods and times to discuss problem solving so that the couple can continue to attend to the business of running a family, for example. Boundaries need to be agreed concerning what, if anything, will be disclosed to children, extended family and friends regarding the current situation. In cases of partner psychological or physical abuse, boundary setting will be primarily focussed on ensuring safety for the injured partner and may involve separating the partners and dealing with the practicalities of one partner moving to alternative accommodation.

Gaining understanding

A key task is to help the couple place the event into an understandable context. A great deal of cognitive and emotional work may be necessary for both partners at this stage. The injured partner may often experience a high degree of rumination about the infidelity and question their partner incessantly about what occurred and why they behaved as they did. Even as the degree of emotional dysregulation subsides and partners experience some sense of 'moving on', the injured partner is likely to experience episodes where their emotional distress is re-triggered. This process can be understood as similar to the experience of 'flashbacks' in trauma reactions, and the couple can be helpfully informed that such experiences may reoccur, even after they have made significant progress, as stimuli are encountered that remind the injured party of the infidelity. Like flashbacks more generally, such experiences are often associated with heightened negative emotional reactions and the couple may feel that 'we are back to where we started'.

In order for the injured partner to move forward in the relationship, they will need to construct a new understanding about their partner and the relationship. The participating partner may also need to gain new understandings about the context for their behaviour and both partners can be significantly helped by a wider understanding of the contextual factors, including characteristics of both partners, their developmental histories and personalities and current and previous environmental contexts that have functioned to increase their vulnerability for an affair to occur. It is essential that the therapist avoid 'blaming the victim' in any explorations of the injured partner's contribution to factors that made the couple vulnerable to the event(s). At the same time, the participating partner continues to be held accountable for their actions, as any formulation of the contributing factors for their behaviour, no matter how complete, does not equate to the behaviour having been 'caused'. Indeed, for many injured partners, experiencing the participating partner take full responsibility for their actions and expressing remorse is a pre-requisite for moving forward. The greater degree of self-understanding created by the formulation of contributing factors ideally assists the partners in becoming more aware of what may need to be attended to in the future in order to prevent similar events occurring.

Moving forward

The final stage involves the partners evaluating their current relationship and coming to a decision about how to move forward either as a couple or separately as individuals. This may involve additional behavioural work on changing patterns that contribute to ongoing vulnerability, where the decision is to remain together. For example, the participating partner may have had to confront relational expectations of 'entitlement' to have needs met or behaviours contributing to poor boundary maintenance. They may need to enact behavioural experiments related to new 'rules for living' in relation to individuals outside of their partnership. Such a behavioural and cognitive shift may be very challenging and require considerable time to become an aspect of that individual's new way of being.

Additional issues include the injured partner rebuilding their sense of trust in the participating partner and moving towards forgiveness. At this stage cognitive and behavioural strategies may be very useful. For example, 'trust', which may be initially expressed in terms of the cognition 'I need to be absolutely certain that you will never do this again', can be re-framed in terms of the 'preparedness to take a reasonable risk in the face of uncertainty'. Similarly, a partner may frame forgiveness unhelpfully as equivalent to 'forgetting' or somehow believing that the behaviour was acceptable or inevitable. Forgiveness may more functionally be defined as 'choosing to move on and giving up the right to continue punishing your partner'. Behavioural experiments may be a strategy of choice to assist partners moving forward with these possibilities.

On other occasions, even after a great deal of work, one or both partners may conclude that the best option they have for meeting their individual needs and goals is to leave the relationship. In this instance CBCT can be focussed on assisting the partners to engage in the process of separation in a manner that is as true to their values as possible and that does the least damage to themselves and other involved individuals such as children.

Ending issues

This chapter focusses on the issue of how therapy might ideally be brought to a close in a manner that is consistent with the principles of CBCT. CBCT values helping clients become their own therapists and attempts to support this by teaching clients skills that will be maintained across time and across situations. This book has frequently emphasised that a central feature of CBCT is flexibility. This ideally extends to the number of treatment sessions that may be offered. Rather than a fixed, one-size-fits-all approach, the therapist should negotiate an initial contract of sessions followed by a review with the option to extend the treatment contract if this looks desirable. A typical 'course' of CBCT may last between 16 and 18 sessions; however, depending upon the complexity of the couple's issues and the range of factors that are involved in the generation of their distress, this can be shorter or considerably longer.

Consistent with its origins in learning theory, CBCT ideally involves the therapist slowly 'fading' the degree of structure and direct support and direct interventions as therapy progresses. As couples move towards the ending stage, they are ideally demonstrating an ability to utilise a range of cognitive, emotional and behavioural skills across different situations and contexts. Evidence that couples are indeed doing so is one way of the therapist assessing the degree to which the therapy may be moving to an appropriate conclusion. Rather than a single 'ending session' which needs to be planned for carefully and which is primarily understood as a separation or loss of the therapeutic relationship, the therapist can plan a number of booster or 'check-in' sessions over several months. This allows a more adequate assessment of the couple's ability to use new skills and also allows for some further problem solving and refinement of changes in the light of new experiences and challenges.

Towards the closing stages of therapy, it can be useful for the therapist and couple to construct a therapy blueprint (Butler et al., 2008). This allows the couple to review the factors that contributed to their distress and also those new skills and cognitive, behavioural and emotional changes that they have made, that have supported them in achieving greater relationship satisfaction. This blueprint can also specify processes, such as a three-monthly 'check in', in which the couple spend some time together to review the extent to which they have remained 'on track' as well as the possibility that they need to consider making further adjustments as they meet new challenges.

Constructing a therapy blueprint for a couple involves asking them to consider a series of questions and formalising their responses in a co-constructed document that can serve as a record of their work together in therapy as well as a useful reminder of those things that they are attempting to carry forward. Useful questions can include (but are not limited to):

- What were the patterns of behaviour for us as individuals and as a couple that led us to experience couple distress?
- What are the normal personality styles and traits that we each possess that have contributed to our difficulties and that we have worked on responding more flexibly to?
- What basic needs and motives have we identified for each of us as individuals and that are important in understanding how our relationship can function more effectively?
- What environmental factors are important in understanding our difficult times as well as our more successful periods?
- What factors in our developmental journey, as individuals and as a couple, also help understand how we ran into difficulties? What challenges may lie ahead?
- What new positive behaviours have we tried and wish to carry forward as part of the way we relate to each other?
- What changes in our beliefs about how our relationship 'should' work have we considered?

ENDING ISSUES

- What new relationship beliefs are we continuing to 'road test' in the months ahead?

Rather than have the couple respond to questions that address all the separate domains discussed in this book, it can be more effective to design a series of questions for each presenting couple based on the assessment and formulation of the main factors involved in the generation and maintenance of their couple distress as well as those interventions, new skills and cognitive changes that they have experienced as being particularly important.

Whilst many couples may achieve good results with CBCT, other couples may end therapy whilst still experiencing significant couple distress. For these couples, an ending process in which the therapist helps the couple gain some understanding of the factors that are continuing to function to maintain couple distress may be useful. Ideally, the therapist will also acknowledge efforts that the couple has made to improve the situation as well as those factors that may have made it difficult for one or both partners to engage fully in the process. Further possibilities for individual therapy or an alternative approach to couple work can then also be considered.

For other couples, the work in therapy has revealed that the chosen direction for one or both partners is to move forward as individuals rather than as a couple. In this case it can be valuable for the therapist to suggest that they continue to attend couple sessions for a period of time, rather than to end at the point at which they have decided that the best decision is to separate. Here, the goal becomes not one of improving couple satisfaction, but supporting a process of separation that acknowledges the value and significance that this relationship has held for both individuals and that also allows for the various steps and challenges of separation to be negotiated and met in a way that causes the least degree of additional emotional distress as possible. Such sessions may often be challenging for both individuals and the therapist as they struggle with feelings of loss, sadness and anger. Indeed, outcome monitoring scales used at this stage may reveal heightened experiences of anxiety or low mood for one or both partners. To regard these increases in symptoms scores as evidence of treatment 'failure' would be too narrow an interpretation in many cases. Many of the skills used in CBCT can be helpful in supporting the individuals to experience, express and regulate these feelings and to make sense of what has happened and move forward as individuals.

30

Conclusion: the challenges and possibilities of CBCT

In this closing chapter I wish to consider some of the significant challenges involved for those therapists new to couple work and/or new to CBCT, as well as some of the advantages and possibilities for therapists incorporating CBCT into their professional skill set.

Possibilities

Individual psychopathology and couple distress are often entwined and mutually reinforcing. For the CBT therapist skilled at offering evidence-based interventions to individual clients, CBCT provides a conceptual framework and a set of powerful interventions that can help significantly widen the range of treatment options. These options can range from partner-assisted interventions to disorder-specific couple-focussed interventions and formal couple therapy, where the aim is to reduce individual psychopathology via improvements in couple functioning and satisfaction. Given that there is evidence that a distressed relationship can function as a vulnerability factor, a trigger factor and maintenance factor for individual psychopathology, as well as a risk factor for relapse following individual therapy, attending to couple issues offers the possibility of enhancing clinical effectiveness and outcome for clients. Services focussed upon providing evidence-based interventions for individual adult clients can be significantly enhanced and potentially achieve greater clinical impact by incorporating couple-based interventions as part of the service offering. For disorders such as depression, where there is a high risk for relapse even after successful CBT, the availability of therapists who can offer CBCT has the potential to improve long-term outcomes.

Challenges

Undoubtedly, one source of challenge can be the wide range of factors that the model suggests can be of relevance in understanding and treating couple distress. Rather than attempting to conduct an exhaustive assessment of all areas identified as of potential relevance in CBCT, followed by an intervention that covers all these bases, therapists often find that couples will present with concerns in several specific domains that can be usefully targeted in treatment. The highly interactive relationship between cognitions, behaviours, emotions and context is such that changes in one domain often result in changes in other domains without these being explicitly targeted.

Work with couples is often demanding and challenging for the therapist. One source of such challenges is that the therapist is required to keep the theoretical model 'in mind' whilst also paying attention to the couple's interaction and each individual's current state (as well as their own) during the session. This is cognitively and often emotionally demanding and best suits therapists who enjoy engaging in such complex processing and the challenge of responding flexibly in the moment rather than conducting sessions in a highly planned or pre-programmed manner. CBCT also asks therapists to take on a wider range of roles than individually focussed forms of CBT and to become comfortable in shifting roles as the need arises. The therapist must be comfortable in the roles of relationship coach/consultant, director, collaborator and empathic, emotionally attuned therapist. For therapists new to work with couples, the demand to institute and maintain an appropriate degree structure in sessions is an important early competence to work on. Therapists can err either on the side of being too directive and structured, such that session allows little room for the partners to express and explore their central concerns, or on the side of having too little structure, which can lead to sessions that are unfocussed or in which the emotional and behavioural dysregulation of one or both partners results in little progress being achieved and the therapist feeling overwhelmed and ineffective. Good supervision is essential in assisting new therapists to learn to balance the need for structure with the need for space to explore deeply personal and often emotionally distressing issues. A related challenge is the need to balance attention to each partner as an individual with attention to the relationship. Therapists need to be aware of the pitfalls of becoming aligned with one partner with the other being explicitly or implicitly identified as 'the problem'.

Therapists who are experienced with individual therapy but new to couple work may also find that engaging in CBCT requires them to clarify and potentially challenge some of their own taken-for-granted standards and beliefs regarding relationships. Often, work with individual clients will not have provided a context in which the impact of such therapist beliefs can become foregrounded. For example, in working with 'affair couples', the therapist may have maintained a belief that an incidence of infidelity always reveals that there are problems in the primary relationship. This assumption is inconsistent with empirical findings (Baucom et al., 2009) and cases where a therapist is working with an affair couple, in which both partners report a high degree of satisfaction before the infidelity occurred, may be challenging for the therapist to understand. Additionally, explorations of couple's beliefs about power and equality in relationships may confront the therapist with their own standards in these areas, which they may not have had occasion to reflect upon. In order that therapists avoid unwittingly imposing their own standards and beliefs upon their client, it can be essential that therapists have the opportunity to explore their assumptions and standards in an appropriately supportive and challenging setting. Such settings can include supervision from a more experienced CBCT therapist as well as peer supervision. Personal therapy may also be considered, when the issues revealed are such that a therapeutic context becomes a more appropriate setting for this exploration. This recommendation is consistent with the work of Bennett-Levy (2006) on the importance of 'the person of the therapist' in understanding the processes and stages involved in the development of a therapist's competence and sense of 'self as therapist'.

My experience, and that of my colleagues, in training experienced CBT therapists to provide CBCT has been immensely rewarding and has indicated that many of these therapists, supported by their strong foundations in the principles of cognitive behavioural therapy, are able to develop into competent and effective practitioners of CBCT, and that working with couples becomes a highly valued part of their professional identity. Additionally, therapists from other orientations, either new to couple work or experienced in work with couples from another orientation, also find that CBCT offers them a flexible and comprehensive model from which they are able to offer effective strategies to a wide range of couples.

References

Barbato, A., and D'Avanzo, B. (2008). Efficacy of couple therapy as a treatment for depression: A meta-analysis. *Psychiatric Quarterly*, *79*, 2, 121–132.

Baucom, D. H., and Epstein, N. B. (1990). *Cognitive-Behavioral Marital Therapy*. New York: Brunner/Mazel.

Baucom, D. H., Epstein, N. B., Kirby, J. S., and Falconier, M. K. (2011). Couple therapy: Theoretical perspectives and empirical findings. In D. Barlow (Ed.) *The Oxford Handbook of Clinical Psychology*, pp. 789–809. New York: Oxford University Press.

Baucom, D. H., Epstein, N. B., LaTaillade, J. J., and Kirby, J. S. (2002). Cognitive-behavioral couple therapy. In A. S. Gurman (Ed.) *Clinical Handbook of Couple Therapy* (4th edition), pp. 31–72. New York: Guilford.

Baucom, D. H., Epstein, N. B., and Sullivan, L. J. (2004). Brief couple therapy. In M. Dewan, B. Steenbarger, and R. P. Greenberg (Eds.) *The Art and Science of Brief Therapies*, pp. 189–227. Washington DC: American Psychiatric Publishing.

Baucom, D. H., Shoham, V., Mueser, K. T., Daiuto, A. D., and Stickle, T. R. (1998). Empirically supported couple and family therapies for adult problems. *Journal of Consulting and Clinical Psychology*, *66*, 53–88.

Baucom, D. H., Snyder, D. K., and Gordon, K. C. (2009). *Helping Couples Get Past the Affair: A clinician's guide*. New York: Guilford.

Baucom, D. H., Stanton, S., and Epstein, N. B. (2003). Anxiety disorders. In D. K. Snyder and M. A. Whisman (Eds.) *Treating Difficult Couples: Helping clients with coexisting mental and relationship disorders*, pp. 57–87. Guilford: New York.

REFERENCES

Beach, S. R. H., Dreifuss, J. A., Franklin, K. J., Kamen, C., and Gabriel, B. (2008). Couple therapy and the treatment of depression. In A. S. Gurman (Ed.) *Clinical Handbook of Couple Therapy* (4th edition), pp. 545–566 New York: Guilford.

Beck, A. T. (1988). *Love Is Never Enough*. New York: Harper & Row.

Beck, A. T., Rush, A. J., Shaw, B. F., and Emery, G. (1979). *Cognitive Therapy of Depression*. New York: Guilford.

Beck, J. S. (1996). *Cognitive Therapy: Basics and beyond*. New York: Guilford.

Bennett, L. A., and Wolin, S. J. (1990). Family culture and alcoholism transmission. In R. L. Collins, K. E. Leonard, and J. S. Searls (Eds.) *Alcohol and Family: Research and clinical perspectives*, pp. 194–219. New York: Guilford.

Bennett-Levy, J. (2006). Therapist skills: A cognitive model of their acquisition and refinement. *Behavioural and Cognitive Psychotherapy*, *34*, 57–78.

Bhugra, D., and De Silva, P. (2000). Couple therapy across cultures. *Sexual and Relationship Therapy*, *15*, 183–192.

Bowlby, J. (1989). The role of attachment in personality development and psychopathology. In S. Greenspan and G. Pollock (Eds.) *The Course of Life: Infancy. Vol. I*, pp. 229–270. Madison, CT: International Universities Press.

Butler, G., Fennell, M., and Hackman, A. (2008). *Cognitive-Behavioral Therapy for Anxiety Disorders: Mastering clinical challenges*. New York: Guilford.

Christensen, A., Atkins, D. C., Berns, S., Wheeler, J., Baucom, D. H., and Simpson, L. E. (2004). Traditional versus integrative behavioural couple therapy for significantly and chronically distressed married couples. *Journal of Consulting and Clinical Psychology*, *72*, 176–191.

Christensen, A., Jacobson, N. S., Babcock, J. C. (1995). Integrative behavioural couple therapy. In N. S. Jacobson and A. S. Gurman (Eds.) *Clinical Handbook of Couple Therapy*, pp. 73–106. New York: Guilford.

Dahl, J., Stewart, I., Martell, C., and Kaplan, J. (2013). *ACT and RFT in Relationships: Helping clients deepen intimacy and maintain healthy commitment using acceptance and commitment therapy and relational frame theory*. Oakland, CA: New Harbinger Publications.

Dattilio, F. M. (2010). *Cognitive-Behavioral Therapy with Couples and Families: A comprehensive guide for clinicians*. New York: Guilford.

Epstein, N. B. (1985). Depression and marital dysfunction: Cognitive and behavioural linkages. *International Journal of Mental Health*, *13*, 86–104.

Epstein, N. B., and Baucom, D. H. (2002). *Enhanced Cognitive-Behavioral Therapy for Couples: A contextual approach*. Washington, DC: American Psychological Association.

REFERENCES

Fischer, M. S., Baucom, D. H., Hahlweg, K., and Epstein, N. B. (2014). Couple therapy. In W. Rief (Ed.) *The Wiley Handbook of Cognitive Behavioral Therapy. Vol II*, pp. 703–726. West Sussex: Wiley-Blackwell.

Flores, E., Tschann, J. M., VanOss Marin, B., and Pantoja, P. (2004). Marital conflict and acculturation among Mexican American husbands and wives. *Cultural Diversity and Ethnic Minority Psychology 10*, 1, 39–52.

Fowers, B. J. (2001). The limits of a technical concept of a good marriage: Examining the role of virtues in communication skills. *Journal of Marital and Family Therapy, 27*, 327–340.

Fruzzetti, A. E. (2012). *The High-Conflict Couple: A dialectical behaviour therapy guide to finding peace, intimacy and validation*. Oakland, CA: New Harbinger Publications.

Fruzzetti, A. E., and Fantozzi, B. (2008). Couple therapy and the treatment of borderline personality and related disorders. In A. S. Gurman (Ed.) *Clinical Handbook of Couple Therapy* (4th edition), pp. 567–590. New York: Guilford.

Gehart, D. R. (2012). *Mindfulness and Acceptance in Couple and Family Therapy*. New York: Springer.

Gordon, K. C., and Baucom, D. H. (1998). A multitheoretical intervention for promoting recovery from extramarital affairs. *Clinical Psychology: Science and practice, 6*, 382–399.

Gordon, K. C., Baucom, D. H., Snyder, D. K., and Dixon, L. J. (2008). Couple therapy and the treatment of affairs. In A. S. Gurman (Ed.) *Clinical Handbook of Couple Therapy* (4th edition), pp. 429–458. New York: Guilford.

Gottman, J. M. (1979). *Marital Interaction: Experimental investigations*. New York: Academic Press.

Gottman, J. M. (1994). *Why Marriages Succeed or Fail*. New York: Simon & Schuster.

Greenberg, L. S., and Goldman, R. N. (2008). *Emotion-Focussed Couples Therapy: The dynamics of emotion, love and power*. Washington, DC: American Psychological Association.

Gurman, A. S. (2008). A framework for the comparative study of couple therapy: History, models, and applications. In A. S. Gurman (Ed.) *Clinical Handbook of Couple Therapy* (4th edition), pp. 1–26. New York: Guilford.

Hahlweg, K., Baucom, D. H., Grawe-Gerber, M., and Snyder, D. K. (2010). Strengthening Couples and Families: Dissemination of interventions for the treatment and prevention of couple distress. In K. Hahlweg, M. Grawe-Gerber and D. H. Baucom (Eds.) *Enhancing Couples: The shape of couple therapy to come*, pp. 3–30. Cambridge, MA: Hogrefe.

REFERENCES

Halford, W. K. (2001). *Brief Therapy for Couples: Helping partners help themselves*. New York: Guilford.

Halford, W. K., Bouma, R., Kelly, A. B., and Young, R. (1999). The interaction of individual psychopathology and marital problems: Current findings and clinical implications. *Behavior Modification*, *23*, 179–216.

Harris, R. (2009). *ACT with Love*. Oakland, CA: New Harbinger Publications.

Hayes, S. C., Strosahl, K. D., and Wilson, K. G. (1999). *Acceptance and Commitment Therapy: An experiential approach to behavior change*. New York: Guilford.

Hays, P. A. (1996). Cultural considerations in couple therapy. *Women and Therapy*, *19*, 3, 13–23.

Hinton, D. E., and La Roche, E. (2014). Cultural context. In S. Hofmann (Ed.) *The Wiley Handbook of Cognitive Behavioral Therapy. Vol I*, pp. 399–433. West Sussex: Wiley-Blackwell.

Jacobson, N. S., and Christensen, A. (1996). *Acceptance and Change in Couple Therapy: A therapist's guide to transforming relationships*. New York: Norton.

Jacobson, N. S., and Margolin, G. (1979). *Marital Therapy: Strategies based on social learning and behavior exchange principles*. New York: Brunner/Mazel.

Jacobson, N. S., and Moore, D. (1981). Spouses as observers of the events in their relationship. *Journal of Consulting and Clinical Psychology*, *49*, 269–277.

Johnson, S. M. (2004). *The Practice of Emotionally Focussed Couple Therapy: Creating connection* (2nd edition). New York: Brunner-Routledge.

Johnson, S. M., and Greenberg, L. S. (1985). Emotionally focussed couples therapy: An outcome study. *Journal of Marital and Family Therapy*, *11*, 313–317.

Johnson, S. M., and Greenberg, L. S. (1995). The emotionally focussed approach to problems in adult attachment. In N. S. Jacobson and A. S. Gurman (Eds.) *Clinical Handbook of Couple Therapy*, pp. 121–141. New York: Guilford.

Kirby, J. S., and Baucom, D. H. (2007). Integrating dialectical behaviour therapy and cognitive-behavioral couple therapy: A couples skills group for emotional dysregulation. *Cognitive and Behavioral Practice*, *14*, 394–405.

LaTaillade, J. J. (2006). Considerations for treatment of African American couple relationships. *Journal of Cognitive Psychotherapy: An international quarterly*, *4*, 341–358.

Leahy, R. (1997). *Practicing Cognitive Therapy: A guide to interventions*. Northvale, NJ: Jason Aronson.

REFERENCES

Leahy, R (2002). A model of emotional schemas. *Cognitive and Behavioural Practice*, 9, 177–190.

Lee, E., and Mock, M. R. (2005). Asian families: An overview. In M. McGoldrick, J. Giordano, and N. Garcia-Preto (Eds.) *Ethnicity and Family Therapy*, pp. 269–289. New York: Guilford.

Linehan, M. M. (1993). *Cognitive-Behavioral treatment of Borderline Personality Disorder*. New York: Guilford.

Long, J. K., and Andrews, B. V. (2011). Fostering strength and resilience in same-sex couples. In J. L. Wetchler (Ed.) *Handbook of Clinical Issues in Couple Therapy*, pp. 225–246. New York: Routledge.

Markus, H. R., and Kitayama, S. (1991). Culture and the self: Implicatons for cognition, emotion, and motivation. *Psychological Review*, 98, 224–253.

McClelland, D. C. (1987). *Human Motivation*. Cambridge: Cambridge University Press.

Minuchin, S. (1974). *Families and Family Therapy*. Cambridge, MA: Harvard University Press.

Moran, D. (2000). *Introduction to Phenomenology*. London: Routledge.

Nichols, M. P., and Schwartz, R. C. (2001). *Family Therapy: Concepts and methods*. Boston, MA: Allyn & Bacon.

Sevier, M., and Jean, C. Y. (2009). Cultural considerations in evidence-based traditional and integrative behavioural couple therapy. In M. Rastogi, and V.Thomas (Eds.) *Multicultural Couple Therapy*. London: Sage.

Snyder, C. R., and Lopez, S. J. (2007). *Positive Psychology: The scientific and practical explorations of human strengths*. London: Sage.

Snyder, D. K. (1979). Multidimensional assessment of marital satisfaction. *Journal of Marriage and the Family*, 41, 813–823.

Snyder, D. K., Castellani, A. M., and Whisman, M. A. (2006). Current status and future directions in couple therapy. *Annual Review of Psychology*, 57, 317–344.

Snyder, D. K., Schneider, W. J., and Castellani, A. M. (2003). Tailoring couple therapy to individual differences: A conceptual approach. In D. K. Snyder, and M. A Whisman (Eds.) *Treating Difficult Couples: Helping clients with coexisting mental and relationship disorders*, pp. 27–52. New York: Guilford.

Snyder, D. K., and Whisman, M. A. (Eds.) (2003). *Treating Difficult Couples: Helping clients with coexisting mental and relationship disorders*. New York: Guilford.

Snyder, D. K., and Wills, R. M. (1989). Behavioral versus insight-oriented marital therapy: Effects on individual and interspousal functioning. *Journal of Consulting and Clinical Psychology*, 57, 39–46.

Spanier, G. B. (1976). Measuring dyadic adjustment: New scales for assessing the quality of marriage and similar dyads. *Journal of Marriage and the Family*, *38*, 15–28.

Spinelli, E. (2007). *Practicing Existential Psychotherapy: The relational world*. London: Sage.

Straus, M. A., Hamby, S. L., Boney-McCoy, S., and Sugarman, D. B. (1996). The revised conflict tactics scales (CTS2): Development and preliminary psychometric data. *Journal of Family Issues*, *17*, 283–316.

Stuart, R. B. (1969). Operant interpersonal treatment for marital discord. *Journal of Consulting and Clinical Psychology*, *33*, 675–682.

Vera, M., Vila, D., Alegria, M. (2002). Cognitive-Behavioral Therapy: Concepts, issues, and strategies for practice with racial/ethnic minorities. In G. Bernal, J. E. Trimble, A. K. Burlew, and F. T. Leong (Eds.) *The Handbook of Racial and Ethnic Minority Psychology*, pp. 521–538. Thousand Oaks, CA: Sage.

Whisman, M. A., and Baucom, D. H. (2012). Intimate relationships and psychopathology. *Clinical Child and Family Psychology Review*, *15*, 4–13.

Whisman, M. A., Dixon, A. E., and Johnson, B. (1997). Therapist's perspectives of couple problems and treatment issues in couple therapy. *Journal of Family Psychology*, *11*, 361–366.

Whisman, M. A., and Uebelacker, L. A. (2003). Comorbidity of relationship distress and mental and physical health problems. In D. K. Snyder and M. A. Whisman (Eds.) *Treating Difficult Couples: Helping clients with coexisting mental and relationship disorders*, pp. 3–26. New York: Guilford

Wile, D. B. (1993). *Couples Therapy: A non-traditional approach*. New York: John Wiley and Sons.

Wright, D. W., Nelson, B. S., and Gergen, K. E. (1994). Marital problems. In P. C. McKenry and S. J. Price (Eds.) *Families and Change: Coping with stressful events*, pp. 40–65. Thousand Oaks, CA: Sage.

Young, J. E. (1990). *Cognitive Therapy for Personality Disorders: A schema focussed approach*. Sarasota, FL: Professional Resource Press.

Index

abuse 3, 20, 77, 78, 108, 121, 122
acceptance and commitment therapy (ACT) 9, 84
achievement motives 37, 85
active-directive therapist style 5–6, 48, 72
activity scheduling 41
adaptation 39, 40, 61, 62, 63, 65
'Adaptation Model' 61
affairs 78, 131; *see also* infidelity
affective reconstruction 11
affiliation 36, 57
aggression 20
agreeableness 38
altruism 36
Andrews, B. V. 51
anger 17, 31, 33, 37, 71, 119
anxiety 3, 31, 33, 37, 47, 54
approach motives 36
arguing 17
Asian cultures 48
assessment 14, 49, 53, 75–78, 85
assumptions 23, 27–28, 101, 114, 116; cognitive therapy 8; emotion schemas 34; 'horizon' concept 47, 61–63; shattered by infidelity 121; therapist's own 131
atmosphere 19, 54–55, 83
attachment 10, 33
attention, selective 8, 24, 25, 97, 99, 114
attributions 8, 24–25, 27, 55, 79, 99, 114, 116, 117
autonomy 5, 35, 36–37, 85, 115
avoidance behaviours 54
avoidance motives 36

balance: communication skills 89; in a relationship 66; therapist's role 71, 73–74
Baucom, D. H. 9, 17, 63; 'Adaptation Model' 61; assumptions 27–28; behavioural strategies 83; boundary maintenance 41; communication 87; decision-making

conversations 93, 95; dialectical behaviour therapy 107–108; emotions 31, 33; environmental factors 43, 44, 109; Family Therapy 40; feedback 79; guided discovery 98; interventions 114, 115–116, 118; motives 35–36, 37; personality traits 37; positive and negative behaviours 18, 19; psychopathology 54; relational schematic processing 29–30, 49; relationship standards 28, 102; Systems Theory 39; therapist's roles 71–72
Beck, A. T. 8, 55
behaviour change 83–85, 99, 111, 114, 117, 119, 122, 124
behavioural activation 85, 119
behavioural couple therapy (BCT) 7–8, 39, 84, 110
behavioural experiments 84, 97, 111, 115–116, 124
behavioural interaction patterns 20–21
beliefs 23, 27–28, 55, 79, 111, 120; cognitive therapy 8; cultural factors 15, 48; emotions 34; exploration of new 116; 'horizon' concept 47, 61–63; parenting 109; schemas 8–9; standards 28, 102; therapist's own 131; therapy blueprint 126; *see also* assumptions
Bennett-Levy, J. 131–132
Bhugra, D. 48–49
blame 25, 74, 93, 109, 110, 123
blueprints 126
borderline personality disorder 55–56

boundary maintenance 40–41, 44, 124
boundary setting 122

catastrophising 8, 97
Christensen, A. 9, 33, 115
cognitions 23–25, 27–30, 34, 55, 114, 130; aims of CBCT 66; behavioural strategies 83; challenging 97–99, 101–104; environmental demands and resources 45–46; interventions 119–120
cognitive behavioural couple therapy (CBCT) 4–5; acceptance 9; assessment 75; behaviour change 83–85; boundary maintenance 41; challenges 130–132; cognitions 23–25, 27–30, 101; cultural factors 47–49; depression 59; difference 47; ending therapy 125; enhancements to 13–16; environmental factors 43, 109–111; needs and goals 39; possibilities 129–130; problematic couple interactions 35; same-sex couples 50–51; separation 124, 128; values and aims 65–67
cognitive behavioural therapy (CBT): cognitions 97, 101; cultural factors 47; problematic couple interactions 35; resilience 15; therapist's role 73
cognitive dissonance 99
cognitive therapy 8
commitment 3
communication 3, 17–18, 116; balanced relationships 66;

behavioural couple therapy 7; communication training 41, 48, 87–91, 93–96, 110–111, 119; decision-making conversations 58, 93–96, 110; emotional expression 34; emotion-focussed couple therapy 10; impact of depression on 58; negative behaviours 19, 20; sharing thoughts and feelings conversations 58, 87–91, 99, 105–106
communion 36, 39
community support 45
compartmentalisation 119
confidentiality 78
conflict 37
Conflict Tactic Scale (CTS2) 77
connection 31, 33, 36, 58
conscientiousness 38
contempt 19, 33
contextual model of couple functioning 15–16, 61–63
control 3, 33
conversations: decision-making 58, 93–96, 110; interventions, 119 120; sharing thoughts and feelings 58, 87–91, 99, 105–106
coping strategies 56
'couple days' 84, 85
couple distress 3–5, 8; assumptions 28; attachment needs 10; cognitive processes 23; contempt and criticism 33; contextual model of couple functioning 63; depression 57–59; emotions 31, 34; ending therapy 127; environmental factors 44; ethnic minorities 49; needs and goals 39; primary and secondary 4–5, 113, 114–116; psychopathology 53, 54–56, 129; same-sex couples 51; therapist's role 71
criticism 19, 20, 32–33
culture 15, 46, 47–49, 106

Dattilio, F. M. 8
De Silva, P. 48–49
decision-making conversations 58, 93–96, 110
defensiveness 32, 98
demands: contextual model of couple functioning 61, 62, 63; environmental 43–44, 45–46, 110, 116
demand-withdraw interactions 20, 35, 78; decision-making conversations 93; feedback from therapist 81; gender differences 50; interventions 115
depression 3, 31, 57–59, 121, 129–130; attributions 25; cultural factors 47; efficacy of couple therapy for 4; feedback from therapist 80–81; interventions 117–120
detachment 31
developmental histories 11, 14, 32, 102, 123
dialectical behaviour therapy (DBT) 107–108
dichotomous thinking 97
difference 47–51, 115
disengagement 3, 21, 32, 71, 76
disgust 19
disorder-specific couple interventions 118–120, 129
distorted cognitions 97, 98, 101
divorce 3; *see also* separation

INDEX

'Downward Arrow' technique 101
Dyadic Adjustment Scale (DAS) 76–77

emotional disengagement 3, 21, 32, 71, 76
emotional support 57–58, 65
emotion-focussed couple therapy (EFCT) 10
emotion-focussed therapy (EFT) 13, 33, 105
emotions 10, 13, 31–38, 130; aims of CBCT 66; behavioural strategies 83; cognitions and 34; communication training 88, 89; emotion schemas 34; emotional experience 31–32, 105–106, 107; expression of 33–34, 48, 105–106, 107, 114, 119; hard and soft 33; infidelity 121, 122, 123; interventions 114, 119; primary and secondary 33; regulation of 32–33, 34, 56, 108, 114; working with 105–108
ending a relationship 67, 124, 127–128
ending therapy 125–128
environment 14–15, 43–46, 109–111, 123, 126
Epstein, N. B. 9, 17, 63; 'Adaptation Model' 61; behavioural strategies 83; boundary maintenance 41; communication 87; decision-making conversations 93, 95; emotions 31, 33; environmental factors 43, 44, 109; Family Therapy 40; feedback 79; guided discovery 98; interventions 114, 115, 118; motives 35–36, 37; personality traits 37; positive and negative behaviours 18, 19; relational schematic processing 29–30, 49; relationship standards 28, 102; Systems Theory 39
equality 28–29, 66, 94, 111, 120, 131
ethnicity 47–49
evidence-based interventions 129
Exchange Theory 7
'existential tension' 103
expectancies 25, 27
expectations 111, 120, 124; cultural factors 15, 46, 48; parenting 109; psychopathology 55; relationship standards 101, 102–103; *see also* beliefs
extended family 43, 44, 59, 85, 110; boundary setting 122; cultural factors 46, 48
extroversion 38, 106–107

Family Therapy 40
feedback 79–82
financial support 44, 45
flashbacks 123
flexibility 5, 63, 71–73, 125, 130
forgiveness 124
formal couple therapy 120, 129
Fowers, B. J. 48

gender 47, 49–50, 102
goals 67, 73, 82
Gordon, K. C. 27–28, 121
Gottman, J. M. 32–33
Greenberg, L. S. 10, 33
guided behaviour change 83–85, 99, 111, 114, 117, 119, 122, 124
guided discovery 98–99

INDEX

guilt 31, 121
Gurman, A. S. 3

Hahlweg, K. 3
Halford, W. K. 61
hard and soft emotions 33
Hays, P. A. 47–48
homeostasis 39, 43–44, 54
homework 7, 73, 116
hopelessness 25
'horizon' concept 47, 61–63, 109
hostility 5, 19, 31, 55, 97–98; decision-making conversations 93; patterns of 114; therapist's role 71, 72

individual therapy 47, 78, 97, 108, 120, 127
individuation 36
infidelity 3, 28, 121–124, 131
information processing 29–30, 49–50, 66, 114
insight-oriented couple therapy (IOCT) 10–11, 14
instrumental behaviours 18
instrumental support 45, 57–58, 65, 120
integrative behavioural couple therapy (IBCT) 9
interventions: communication training 41, 48, 87–91, 93–96, 110–111, 119; guided behaviour change 83–85, 99, 111, 114, 117, 119, 122, 124; guided discovery 98–99; psychopathology 117–120, 129; sequencing 113–116
interviews 75–76, 78
intimacy 35, 36, 57, 58, 115
introversion 38, 106–107

Jacobson, N. S. 9, 24, 115
jealousy 31
Jean, C. Y. 48
Johnson, S. M. 10, 33

Kirby, J. S. 107
kissing 19

Leahy, R. 34
listening skills 90, 99, 119
Long, J. K. 51
love 31

macro level factors 13–14, 39–41, 63, 67, 73, 99
Marital Satisfaction Inventory (MSI) 76–77
McClelland, D. C. 35
micro level factors 7, 13–14, 17–21, 39, 41, 63, 67, 73
mindfulness 9
'mini-talks' 98, 105
Minuchin, S. 40–41
Moore, D. 24
motives 4–5, 35–37, 85, 115–116, 120, 126
moving forward 124
mutual attack 20
mutual disengagement 21

needs 4–5, 14, 39, 45, 85, 115–116, 120, 126; *see also* motives
negative affectivity 31–32
negative behaviours 15, 17, 19–20; attributions 25; behavioural couple therapy 7; cognitions 99; guided behaviour change 83; selective attention 24; therapist's role 72

143

negative reciprocity 20, 25, 35, 78, 109, 119
neuroticism 38
non-communication behaviours 18
number of sessions 82, 125

observation 77–78
obsessive compulsive disorder 54
openness to experience 38

parenting 109, 111
partner-assisted interventions 117–118, 129
personality 14, 37–38, 104, 115, 126
personality disorders 55–56
phobias 54
positive affectivity 31
positive behaviours 15–16, 17, 18–19, 126; attributions 25; behavioural activation 119; behavioural couple therapy 7; guided behaviour change 84, 85
Positive Psychology 15
positive reciprocity 20
power 3, 102, 120, 131; cultural factors 48; demand-withdraw interactions 50; emotions 33; equal balance of 66; motives 37; unequal distribution of 111
primary distress 4–5, 113, 115–116
primary emotions 33
problem solving 87, 93–96, 110, 120, 122
psychodynamic approaches 11
psychoeducation 72, 111, 116, 118, 122
psychopathology 3–4, 14, 23, 53–56; assessment of 78; dysregulation of emotions 13; interventions 117–120, 129; maintenance of 35; negative behaviours 20; schemas 29, 34; *see also* depression

questionnaires 76–77

racism 49
reciprocity, negative 20, 25, 35, 78, 109, 119
relational schematic processing 29–30, 49–50, 66, 114
relationship-oriented standards 28–29, 66, 101–104
resilience 15, 63, 66, 110
resources 43–45, 61, 63, 76, 110, 111, 116
'response-delay' strategies 108
rituals 40, 44, 45
role conflicts 3
role-reversal exercises 120
rules: for behaviour 23; emotion schemas 34; for living 124
rumination 57, 58, 123

sadness 31
same-sex couples 3, 50–51, 63, 66
sarcasm 20, 81, 83
'Schema Focussed Therapy' 29
schemas 8–9, 29–30, 34, 55, 56; *see also* relational schematic processing
'schematic model' 61
secondary distress 5, 113, 114–115
secondary emotion 33
selective attention 8, 24, 25, 97, 99, 114
self-efficacy 115, 120

INDEX

self-esteem 19, 44, 55
self-report questionnaires 76–77
self-soothing 108
self-talk 98
separateness motives 36
separation 124, 127–128
sequencing interventions 113–116
sessions: focus of 72–73, 130; number of 82, 125
Sevier, M. 48
sexual issues 3
sexual orientation 47, 50–51
shame 31, 33, 48, 59
sharing thoughts and feelings conversations 58, 87–91, 99, 105–106
skills 114, 125; behavioural strategies 7–8, 83; communication 87–91, 95, 116, 119; parenting 111; problem-solving 110; therapist's role 72, 73
social cognition 8–9
Social Learning Theory 7
social support 41, 45, 117, 119–120
Socratic Dialogue 97, 98
speaking skills 88–90
stability 39, 40
standards 28–29, 59, 66, 101–104, 114; boundary maintenance 41; cultural factors 48; emotion schemas 34; exploration of new 116; therapist's own 131
stonewalling 32
stress 14, 44, 55, 65, 111
stressors 49, 53, 55, 56, 76
structure 130–131
Stuart, R. B. 7
substance misuse 3
succorance 36

suicide 117–118
supervision 131
systemic models 15
Systems Theory 10, 39, 43

temperament 14, 116
therapeutic relationship 48–49, 66, 73, 125
therapists: active-directive therapist style 5–6, 48, 72; aims and goals of therapy 66–67; assessment by 49, 75–78, 85; challenges for 130–132; challenging cognitions 97–99; communication training 87–91, 95–96; cultural factors 48–49; ending therapy 125–126; feedback from 79–82; role and stance of 71–74; working with emotions 105–107
therapy blueprints 126
thought diaries 97
trauma 54, 121, 123
trust 124
turn taking 93

unilateral disengagement 21

values 3, 28–29, 47–48
verbal threats 20
virtues 48

well-being 3, 28
withdrawal 5, 20–21, 35, 44, 78; decision-making conversations 93; depression 57; feedback from therapist 81; gender differences 50; interventions 115

Young, Jeffery 29

eBooks
from Taylor & Francis

Helping you to choose the right eBooks for your Library

Add to your library's digital collection today with Taylor & Francis eBooks. We have over 50,000 eBooks in the Humanities, Social Sciences, Behavioural Sciences, Built Environment and Law, from leading imprints, including Routledge, Focal Press and Psychology Press.

Choose from a range of subject packages or create your own!

Benefits for you
- Free MARC records
- COUNTER-compliant usage statistics
- Flexible purchase and pricing options
- All titles DRM-free.

Benefits for your user
- Off-site, anytime access via Athens or referring URL
- Print or copy pages or chapters
- Full content search
- Bookmark, highlight and annotate text
- Access to thousands of pages of quality research at the click of a button.

Free Trials Available
We offer free trials to qualifying academic, corporate and government customers.

eCollections

Choose from over 30 subject eCollections, including:

Archaeology	Language Learning
Architecture	Law
Asian Studies	Literature
Business & Management	Media & Communication
Classical Studies	Middle East Studies
Construction	Music
Creative & Media Arts	Philosophy
Criminology & Criminal Justice	Planning
Economics	Politics
Education	Psychology & Mental Health
Energy	Religion
Engineering	Security
English Language & Linguistics	Social Work
Environment & Sustainability	Sociology
Geography	Sport
Health Studies	Theatre & Performance
History	Tourism, Hospitality & Events

For more information, pricing enquiries or to order a free trial, please contact your local sales team:
www.tandfebooks.com/page/sales

www.tandfebooks.com